# THE COMPLETE ILLUSTRATED GUIDE TO THE
# CATHOLIC FAITH

## BELIEF · PRAYER · RITUAL · SACRAMENTS · WORSHIP

Examines the institutions of the Church and explores the significance of the sacraments, with over 180 photographs · Charles Phillips CONSULTANT: Reverend Ronald Creighton-Jobe

southwater

This edition is published by Southwater,
an imprint of Anness Publishing Ltd,
Blaby Road, Wigston,
Leicestershire LE18 4SE

info@anness.com

www.southwaterbooks.com;
www.annesspublishing.com

Anness Publishing has a new picture agency outlet for images for publishing, promotions or advertising. Please visit our website www.practicalpictures.com for more information.

## ETHICAL TRADING POLICY

At Anness Publishing we believe that business should be conducted in an ethical and ecologically sustainable way, with respect for the environment and a proper regard to the replacement of the natural resources we employ.

As a publisher, we use a lot of wood pulp in high-quality paper for printing, and that wood commonly comes from spruce trees. We are therefore currently growing more than 750,000 trees in three Scottish forest plantations: Berrymoss (130 hectares/320 acres), West Touxhill (125 hectares/305 acres) and Deveron Forest (75 hectares/185 acres). The forests we manage contain more than 3.5 times the number of trees employed each year in making paper for the books we manufacture.

Because of this ongoing ecological investment programme, you, as our customer, can have the pleasure and reassurance of knowing that a tree is being cultivated on your behalf to naturally replace the materials used to make the book you are holding.

Our forestry programme is run in accordance with the UK Woodland Assurance Scheme (UKWAS) and will be certified by the internationally recognized Forest Stewardship Council (FSC). The FSC is a non-government organization dedicated to promoting responsible management of the world's forests. Certification ensures forests are managed in an environmentally sustainable and socially responsible way. For further information about this scheme, go to www.annesspublishing.com/trees

Previously published as part of a larger volume, *The Illustrated Encyclopedia of Catholicism*

Publisher: Joanna Lorenz
Editorial Director: Helen Sudell
Editor: Elizabeth Young
Cover Design: Lesley Mitchell
Production Controller: Bessie Bai

Produced for Anness Publishing by Toucan Books:
Managing Director: Ellen Dupont
Editor: Theresa Bebbington
Project Manager: Hannah Bowen
Designer: Elizabeth Healey
Picture Researcher: Marian Pullen
Proofreader: Marion Dent
Indexer: Michael Dent
Cartography by Cosmographics, UK

## PUBLISHER'S NOTE

Although the advice and information in this book are believed to be accurate and true at the time of going to press, neither the authors nor the publisher can accept any legal responsibility or liability for any errors or omissions that may have been made.

## PICTURE CREDITS

The publishers have made every effort to trace the photograph copyright owners. Anyone we have failed to reach is invited to contact Toucan Books, 89 Charterhouse Street, London EC1M 6HR, United Kingdom.
akg-images 32tr, 38tr, 39br, 50tr, 50b, 60bl, 69br, 81tl, 92br, 93tl. Alamy 4–5, 11br, 16bl, 20tr and 20br, 26t, 27b, 29tr, 29br, 30t, 31t, 32bl, 38bl, 39tm, 41bl, 42bl, 43br, 44bl, 45rm, 47bl, 49bl, 54tr, 54bl, 59br, 60tr, 62bl, 64tr, 64bl, 69t, 72b, 75bl, 84tr, 89t, 89br, 91tr. ArkReligion.com 15br, 18t, 18bl, 19tr, 24, 26br, 28bl, 41tl, 43bl, 47tm, 48tr, 52bl, 53br, 82bm. The Art Archive 37tm, 40tr, 41tr, 46bl, 48bl, 52tr, 55tm, 55br, 56bl, 57tr, 57br, 59t, 63b, 66bm, 70bl, br and 71bl, br, 73tr, 73b, 74tr, 77tm, 80tr, 80bm, 82tr, 83b, 85b, 88tr, 90tr, 90bl, 92tr, 92bl, 93tr, 94bl, 94br, 95tl. The Bridgeman Art Library 22tr, 31br, 35br, 42t, 58tr, 61tr, 66t, 67tr, 68b, 72t, 78t, 78b, 81mr, 83tr, 84b, 86t, 88bl. Corbis front cover main image, 8b, 9tr, 10bl, 11tr, 12tr, 14tr, bl, 15bl, 16tr, 21br, 22bl, 23tr and bm, 24tr, 25br, 36–7, 45br, 46tr, 47b, 49tr, 51tr, 53tr, 56tr, 62tr, 65bl, 70tr, 75tm, 76–7, 79br, 86, 87t, 93br. Getty Images 7tm, 8tr, 9br, 12bl, 13mr, 13br, 17tr, 17bl, 19br, 21tl, 34tr, 34bl, 35tm, 51tl, 58bl, 61bl, 67bl, 74bl, 79tr, 81tr, 87br, 91br, 95tr. Courtesy Hayes & Finch 44tr. Kobal Collection 25tr. Photoshot 95bm. Photolibrary 6–7, 27t, 30bl, 40bl, 65tm, 68tr, 81bl, 85t. Robert Harding 28tr, 51br, 81br. TopFoto 33tr and br. Courtesy Vanpoulles Ltd 63tl.

Front cover main image shows Pope Benedict XVI celebrates the midnight Christmas Holy Mass in the Vatican Basilica of Saint Peter. Endpaper shows Saint Peters Dome; the Vatican.

# CONTENTS

Introduction                                        4

## INSTITUTIONS OF THE CHURCH          6
The Holy Father                                     8
The Vatican: A Place Apart                         10
Hierarchy of the Church                            12
The Path to Priesthood                             14
Married to the Church                              16
Called to Serve                                    18
Under Orders                                       20
Brothers in Christ                                 22
A Contemplative Christianity                       24
Working in the World                               26
Brides of Christ                                   28
Living for Others                                  30
The Missions                                       32
Lay Groups                                         34

## LIVING THE SACRAMENTS               36
God's House                                        38
Great Churches                                     40
The Altar of God                                   42
Vestments                                          44
"Gathered Together in My Name"                     46
The Most Holy Sacrament of the Altar               48
Baptism                                            50

Confirmation                                       52
Holy Matrimony                                     54
"What God Has Joined…"                             56
The Sanctity of Life                               58
Penance and Reconciliation                         60
Anointing of the Sick and the Last Rites           62
Dust to Dust                                       64
Prayer                                             66
The Sacred Heart                                   68
Stations of the Cross                              70
The Rosary                                         72
The Blessing                                       74

## THE CATHOLIC YEAR                    76
Holy Days                                          78
The Festive Calendar                               80
A Child Is Born                                    82
Carnival!                                          84
Ash Wednesday and Lent                             86
Holy Week                                          88
The Resurrection and Easter                        90

Chronology of Popes                                92
Religious Orders                                   94

Index                                              96

# INTRODUCTION

One of the world's biggest institutions, the Catholic Church has a spiritual, cultural and historical heritage that spans more than 2000 years. One of the oldest and most practised religions, it has a great influence across the world and a special place in the hearts and minds of millions of people.

This informative book offers a factual account of the Church's rituals and theology. Divided into three sections, the first, Institutions of the Church, looks at how the Catholic doctrines find expression in the everyday life of the Church: in its institutions, its rituals and its festivities. Religious life is examined: the contemplative, the charitable and the missionary vocations; the duties performed by the different sorts of priests and nuns; and the vows such men and women take, along with the reasoning behind them.

This is followed by Living the Sacraments, which describes the rituals of the seven sacraments in detail and what they mean – from baptism to the anointing of the sick, these mark out the landmark moments in the life of the believer, from birth to death.

Finally, The Catholic Year explores the main holy days and the feasts, such as Christmas, Ash Wednesday and Lent, The Resurrection and Easter, their spiritual meanings and the often colourful customs associated with them.

*Left: The Eucharist, along with baptism and confirmation, is a sacrament of initiation into the Catholic Church. These girls are taking their first Holy Communion in Charlotte, North Carolina, in the United States.*

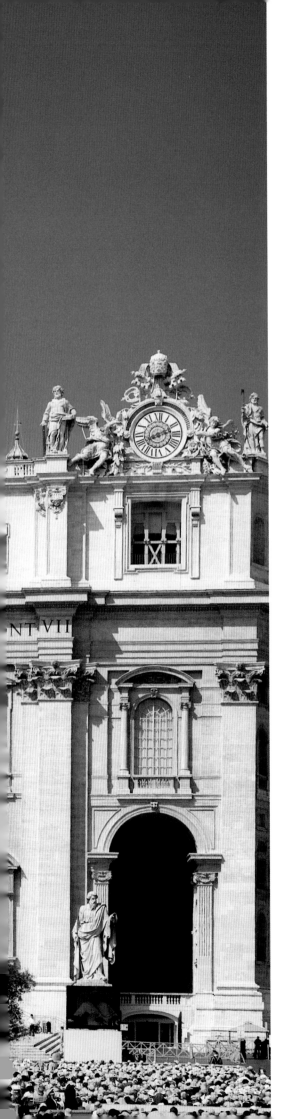

# INSTITUTIONS OF THE CHURCH

On Easter Day, tens of thousands of Roman Catholics pack into St Peter's Square in Vatican City, Rome, to hear the pope celebrate Mass and give his Easter address. The event is broadcast live around the world: the address and the Apostolic blessing that follows it are termed *Urbi et Orbi* ("to the City [of Rome] and to the World").

As spiritual leader of the Roman Catholic Church, the pope heads a vast global organization. Pope Benedict XVI's third Easter address, delivered on 23 March 2008, was televised in 57 countries, and he followed it by giving Easter greetings in no fewer than 63 languages. According to figures released by the Church hierarchy in March 2008, more than one in six people worldwide – 17.4 per cent of the global population – is Roman Catholic. This percentage is equal to around 1.13 billion people.

For these people the pope's authority is supreme. As well as being Europe's only absolute monarch, ruler of Vatican City (the world's smallest independent state), he stands at the head of the Holy See, the Church's machinery of government, and its administrative structure, the Roman Curia. He is at the peak of the great Church hierarchy of cardinals and archbishops, bishops, priests and deacons that also includes the many thousands of priests, monks, friars, nuns and religious sisters in the Church's religious orders. He is nothing less than the Vicar of Christ, his representative on earth. Yet in all these roles, the pope is called to humility and service: among his official titles is "Servant of the Servants of God", in line with the passage in St Matthew's Gospel (20:27) where Christ declares "whoever would be first among you must be your slave".

*Above Standing in the central loggia of St Peter's Basilica, Pope Benedict XVI gives the* Urbi et Orbi *blessing that follows the Easter Sunday Mass.*

*Left A vast crowd of the Roman Catholic faithful attend open-air Mass in St Peter's Square at the Vatican on Easter Sunday.*

# THE HOLY FATHER

THE POPE HAS ULTIMATE AUTHORITY OVER ROMAN CATHOLICS AND OVER THE CHURCH. HE IS ONE OF A LONG SUCCESSION OF POPES, ELECTED TO THIS POSITION BY THE COLLEGE OF CARDINALS.

The title "pope" derives from the words in Late Latin (*papa*) and Greek (*pappas*) meaning "father", and his position is similar to that of a father in a patriarchal family. The pope is addressed as "Your Holiness" and "Holy Father". In addition, the pope has eight formal titles listed in the official directory of the Holy See (the central government of the Catholic Church): Bishop of Rome, Vicar of Jesus Christ, Successor of the Prince of the Apostles, Supreme Pontiff of the Universal Church, Primate of Italy, Archbishop and Metropolitan of the Roman Province, Sovereign of the State of Vatican City and Servant of the Servants of God.

## SUCCESSOR OF ST PETER

Bishop of Rome and Successor of the Prince of the Apostles are two titles that reflect the fact that for Roman Catholics the pope is a spiritual descendant of the apostle St Peter. Pope Benedict XVI, who has been pope from 19 April 2005, is said to be the 265th pope in an unbroken succession of popes from St Peter.

According to biblical accounts, Christ renamed Simon, son of John, Peter, based on the Greek *petros*, or "rock", because the Church was to be built with his strength. In later tradition, Peter was recognized as the leader of the 12 disciples who established the Christian Church in Italy, becoming the first Bishop of Rome. He was also buried in Rome, in the place where the high altar in St Peter's Basilica now stands.

## CHRIST'S REPRESENTATIVE

The pope is also called the Vicar of Christ, meaning his representative – a person acting in his place.

*Below Under rules introduced in 1970 by Pope Paul VI, only cardinals aged 80 or below can vote for a new pope. In 2005, 117 cardinals were eligible to vote when Pope Benedict XVI was elected.*

*Above The name conclave comes from the Latin cum clave ("with a key"). At one time the cardinals were locked away until a new pope was elected.*

For Roman Catholics, the pope serves as Christ's officer, with supreme authority over the Church, because he occupies the place of St Peter, who was originally given the authority to serve in this way. Pope Gelasius I (served AD 492–6) was the first to assume the name "Vicar of Christ"; before his time Christians had reserved the title for the Holy Spirit and popes were referred to as "Vicar of St Peter". The other titles reinforce the pope's position as supreme ruler of both the Catholic Church and the Vatican.

Roman Catholics believe that – just as the pope is the successor of St Peter – the archbishops and bishops of the Church are the successors of the apostles. The archbishops, bishops and the pope receive from the Holy Spirit the gift of infallibility – the capacity to discern what is right, and to be free from mistakes in morals and matters of faith when they jointly proclaim a doctrine. By this remarkable gift they share a part of Christ's own infallibility. The pope as

leader of the bishops possesses a unique infallibility that makes it possible for him to make a definitive decree on doctrine that concerns matters of faith or morals.

## RITUALS OF ELECTION

The pope is elected by the College of Cardinals in a series of closed sessions called a papal conclave, held in the Sistine Chapel in the Vatican Palace. The cardinals vote by writing the name of their preferred candidate on ballot papers beneath the words *Eligo in Summum Pontificem* ("I Elect as Supreme Pontiff"). They carry on voting until one man has the votes of two-thirds of the cardinals plus one. However, if the process becomes prolonged, the cardinals can agree to elect by simple majority.

When one name is agreed, the cardinal in question is asked if he accepts election as Supreme Pontiff. If he replies yes, he then gives the papal name by which he will be known, and the other cardinals pay him their respects.

The pope blesses the crowd and is then ceremonially installed in a service a few days later. At one time this was a grand coronation, but since the time of Pope John Paul I (served for 33 days in 1978), this has been replaced with a simpler ceremony in which the pope is invested with the papal robe, called the pallium, during a Papal Inauguration Mass.

*Above* During a conclave in the Sistine Chapel at the Vatican to appoint a new pope, ballot papers are placed in these ballot boxes by the cardinals.

*Below* Pope John Paul II greets the faithful during his first public appearance at the Vatican after his election to the papacy on 16 October 1978.

# THE VATICAN: A PLACE APART

THE ROMAN CATHOLIC CHURCH'S CENTRE OF GOVERNMENT, GENERALLY KNOWN AS "THE VATICAN", IS IN VATICAN CITY. IT HAS ITS OWN MILITARY CORPS, GOVERNMENT AND INFRASTRUCTURE.

Vatican City is a city-state set within the Italian capital Rome. The world's smallest independent state, the Vatican covers about 44 hectares (109 acres) and has a population of between 800 and 1,000 people. The city-state is mostly enclosed by high stone walls that separate it from Rome. It is the sovereign territory of the Holy See (the Church's central government), and heads the Church's machinery of spiritual and pastoral rule.

While the Holy See has a history dating to the time of St Peter, Vatican City was created only in 1929 under the Lateran Treaty signed by the Kingdom of Italy and the Holy See. Its official name is *Stato della Città del Vaticano* ("the State of Vatican City").

*Below St Peter's Basilica looks down on St Peter's Square. The basilica's majestic 45m (150ft)-high façade was built by Carlo Maderno in the 17th century.*

Vatican City is run as an elected monarchy that is ruled by the pope. One of the pope's formal titles is Sovereign of the State of Vatican City. Roman Catholic clergymen serve as the city-state's chief functionaries. The official state flag is the yellow and white papal banner.

## MOUNT VATICAN

Vatican City takes its name from the hill in north-western Rome on which it stands. This area was known as *Mons Vaticanus* ("Mount Vatican") by the Romans in the pre-Christian era. The city contains the magnificent domed church of St Peter's Basilica, which by tradition stands over the burial place of St Peter, as well as the vast Vatican Palace (also known as the Apostolic Palace). With more than 1,000 rooms, this is an impressive structure that contains the pope's apartments, the

*Above Indoors, the vast scale of St Peter's Basilica impresses upon worshippers the power and grandeur of God – Father, Son and Holy Spirit.*

Church's government offices and several chapels, as well as the Vatican Museum and the Vatican Library.

Within the complex is the Sistine Chapel, famed for its ceiling frescoes of scenes from the book of Genesis that were painted by Michelangelo in 1508–12. It also has a papal reception suite decorated with frescoes by Raphael and the artists of his studio, from 1508 onward, and the Borgia Apartment, a suite decorated with frescoes by Pinturicchio in 1492–5 for Rodrigo Borgia, Pope Alexander VI. The Vatican Museum contains a wealth of statuary, including the ancient Roman statues of *Apollo Belvedere* (350–325 BC) and of *Laocoön and His Sons* (160–20 BC).

Adjacent to the museum, the Vatican Archive houses religious and historical documents dating back over centuries, including the report on the Church trial in 1633 of mathematician and astronomer Galileo Galilei, whose promotion of the theory that Earth and other planets revolve around the Sun was

condemned by the Church on the grounds that it conflicted with Scripture. The complex also holds the Vatican Library, which has one of the world's most valuable collections of manuscripts and early books.

A number of other buildings belong to Vatican City but are situated beyond the city walls. These include the pope's summer villa in Castle Gandolfo, 24km (15 miles) south of Rome, as well as the churches of St John Lateran, St Mary Major and St Paul's Outside the Walls, all in Rome. The Church of St John Lateran is Rome's Cathedral Church and the ecclesiastical seat of the Bishop of Rome – that is, of the pope.

## PROTECTING THE CITY

Vatican City has its own military corps known as the Pontifical Swiss Guard. The guardsmen, who are all Swiss and Roman Catholics, maintain a 24-hour watch over the pope and the Apostolic Palace. The Swiss Guard's role in protecting the pope dates back to the time of Pope Sixtus IV in the late 15th century. The guardsmen wear a Renaissance-style uniform that is sometimes said to have been designed by Michelangelo, but in fact was created in 1914. Technically, the Swiss Guard is a unit of the Holy See, not Vatican City.

The city has its own security and civil defence services department. It encompasses a police and security force called the Gendarme Corps of Vatican City-State, as well as its own fire brigade.

## RUNNING THE CITY

The Vatican has the infrastructure and machinery of government necessary to run an independent country: a diplomatic corps; a court system; its own bank and independent postal,

*Right The elaborate Vatican Library was established by Pope Nicholas V in 1448. It holds some of the most important books from the earliest days of the Church.*

*Above As well as protecting the pope and the Apostolic Palace, the Pontifical Swiss Guard are responsible for controlling access into and out of Vatican City.*

telephone and telegraph services; its own water supply; street-cleaning and lighting; and a railway system. The railway is a stretch of track about 270m (885ft) in length, used for carrying freight. There is even a Vatican jail and a printing plant.

The Pontifical Commission for the State of Vatican City, a group of cardinals appointed by the pope, has responsibility for the state's domestic administration, while foreign relations are handled by the Secretariat of State of the Holy See.

The Vatican City newspaper *L'Osservatore Romano* (The Rome Observer) has been published since 1 July 1861. It was initially independently run, but since 1885 it has been owned by the Holy See.

# HIERARCHY OF THE CHURCH

FROM PAPACY TO PARISH, THE CATHOLIC CHURCH'S HIERARCHY IS A VAST PYRAMID CONNECTING THE POPE AT ITS SUMMIT THROUGH PRIESTS AND DEACONS TO MEMBERS OF THE FAITHFUL AT THE BASE.

As Vicar of Christ on Earth, the pope holds supreme and universal power over the Roman Catholic Church. As Bishop of Rome and successor to St Peter, he is foremost among, and leader of, the bishops of the Church.

### THE UPPER HIERARCHY

Bishops, archbishops and cardinals are at the top of the hierarchy. The pope has ultimate authority for the appointment of bishops. With them he shares what is termed "collegiate" responsibility for leading the Church.

*Below On ordination a bishop becomes a member of the College of Bishops and takes on his share of responsibility for governing the Church.*

The bishops together form the College of Bishops. They are viewed as the successors of Christ's apostles and have a duty to teach the faithful.

Each bishop is in charge of an ecclesiastical area known as a diocese, which contains several individual parishes. His principal task is to care for the faithful in his area, like a shepherd cares for sheep. The main church of the diocese is known as a cathedral and is the ecclesiastical seat (base) of the bishop. In some metropolitan areas, an "ordinary bishop" is the principal bishop and is assisted by a team of auxiliary bishops.

The pope appoints some bishops as archbishops. They have control of an even larger area known as an

*Above Archbishop Egan leads his first service as archbishop in St Patrick's Cathedral, New York, on 19 June 2000. Archbishops are responsible for presiding over Mass in their ecclesiastical seat.*

archdiocese, which contains a number of dioceses. The pope is also responsible for appointing some senior bishops as cardinals. They form the College of Cardinals. Some care for dioceses, while others serve the pope as advisers and administrators in Rome. When a pope dies or if a pope abdicates, the cardinals meet in closed session (conclave) to elect one of their number as the next pope.

### PRIESTS AND DEACONS

Beneath the bishops are two further ranks in the ordained orders: priests and deacons. Priests have the same principal responsibility as a bishop, which is to care for the faithful in the area. Priests proclaim the gospels, lead community prayer and worship, celebrate Mass and the other sacraments for their congregation and teach the faith. Some are members of religious orders, while others are diocesan priests devoted to service in a particular diocese. Most serve in parishes but some instead serve as chaplains in hospitals, universities, prisons or the armed services.

Both priests and bishops are assisted by deacons. In the early Church, deacons also held a special responsibility for charitable work, but as the role of deacon evolved, it became no more than a stage in training to become a priest. However, reforms introduced in 1967 by Pope Paul VI have re-established a group of permanent deacons in the Church. These deacons are men not called to be priests. They often have full-time jobs outside the Church, and whereas priests must be celibate, some deacons may be married.

## WITHIN THE RANKS

Ecclesiastical duties are restricted by rank. Only bishops can perform ordination – that is, make others a bishop, a priest or a deacon through the sacrament of Holy Orders, which is centred on the laying on of hands and a prayer of consecration. Only bishops or priests can say Mass or hear confession.

Deacons have a special responsibility for reading the gospel in Church and for working with the poor. Deacons can preach, perform baptism and conduct marriage services – in the latter case they technically act as witnesses, because the bride and groom administer the sacrament of Holy Matrimony to one other.

## CHURCH GOVERNMENT

The pope is the head of the Holy See, the Church's central machinery of government. The Holy See's administrative structures are collectively known as the Roman Curia. The Roman Curia is divided into several departments, the most important of which is the Secretariat of State, which performs political and diplomatic work for the Holy See.

*Right Pope Benedict XVI presides over the Roman Curia at the Vatican. Curia (from medieval Latin) means "court" – as in "royal court".*

## CANON LAW

The Roman Catholic Church has its own legal system, complete with its courts, judges, lawyers and legal code. The code derives its authority from the council of bishops as descendants of the apostles and the pope as successor of St Peter and Vicar of Christ.

The code has its original source in canons (rules) adopted by Church councils, supplemented by papal decretals or letters that state legal decisions, and input from Celtic, Saxon and other legal traditions. The material was formulated as a code and promulgated by Pope Benedict XV in 1917, then revised in the 1960s to 1980s and repromulgated by Pope John Paul II in 1983.

Parts of the code were adapted from Roman Law as codified on the order of Byzantine emperor Justinian I in AD 529–34. Church courts follow the Roman law style practised in continental Europe, with panels of judges and inquisitorial or investigative proceedings, as distinct from the adversarial proceedings with a single judge and a jury followed in law courts in the United Kingdom and the United States.

*Above A canon law tribunal hears a case. Roman Catholic canon law is the world's oldest continuously used legal system.*

The Secretariat is split into the Section for General Affairs, which holds responsibility for appointments, documents and so on, and the Section for Relations with States. The latter is responsible for interacting with governments of countries from around the world as well as with international bodies, such as the United Nations.

# THE PATH TO PRIESTHOOD

A MAN CALLED TO THE PRIESTHOOD UNDERGOES TRAINING THAT OFTEN TAKES SEVEN OR MORE YEARS AND INCLUDES STUDY IN A SEMINARY AND PASTORAL WORK IN A PARISH.

The journey to the priesthood starts by receiving a call from God to serve as a priest. The calling is known as a vocation (from the Latin *vocatus*, which is the past participle of *vocare*, or "to call"). The call to become a priest is only one of four possible vocations that are recognized by the Roman Catholic Church.

The other three are the calls to life as a brother or sister in a religious order; the call to marriage, with husband and wife sharing faithful love; and the call to single life, embracing celibacy and living either alone, with family or with other single faithful.

These four vocations are viewed as being equal but different. Each faithful Catholic will receive a call by God to one of the four forms of life. The task is to discern the calling and then test it to be sure that a person is

*Below During an ordination service, ordinands prostrate themselves to symbolize their personal unworthiness, humility and reliance on the Grace of God.*

truly being called to that particular pathway. The training to become a priest is known as his formation. The details of the training vary from place to place, but the process typically encompasses several stages.

## PASSING THE TEST

If a young man acts upon a calling to become a priest, he must be willing to embrace a life of celibacy and prayer. He must be ready to commit to proclaiming the gospel, teaching the Catholic faith and doing his utmost to build his faith community. This is a lifelong commitment, so first the young man will need to test his vocation during a period of enquiry and preparation.

He is expected to pray to God for guidance and to be open and patient in waiting for a response. He will discuss his vocation with his local priest and either through him or independently can make contact with the specialist vocations director of the diocese or of a religious order if he feels called to join one.

*Above Young men training for the priesthood pray in a seminary chapel. The word "seminary" comes from the Latin* seminarium *("bed of seeds").*

## EARLY EDUCATION

If he is convinced that he has a vocation, the next stage is to apply to a seminary, a theological college specializing in training priests. A young man who wants to become a diocesan priest applies to a seminary through his local diocese. If he wants to become a priest in a religious order, such as the Franciscans, he applies directly to the order. The application process for a seminary generally includes academic assessment, interviews and psychological tests.

If the young man is accepted into the seminary, he begins his priestly education. The amount of time this takes depends on many factors, including the level of his previous education. His studies will include philosophy, theology, history and Scripture. The training will usually encompass a pre-pastoral stage of study for a year or two, followed by a pastoral stage in which the student serves in a working parish – perhaps returning to his own parish.

## TRANSITIONAL DEACON

The next stage is to train as a deacon. For many years being a deacon was a stage in training to be a priest, but following Pope Paul VI's reforms there has been a return to the practice – common in the early Church – of maintaining a group of permanent deacons who are not destined to be

priests. For this reason, students training to be priests who become deacons are now referred to as transitional deacons to distinguish them from permanent deacons.

After training the student is ordained a deacon. He will then serve for some time – at least six months, but often longer than that – as a transitional deacon before being ordained as a priest.

## CALLED AS A PRIEST

At the completion of his training a student is called to be a priest by his bishop. If the bishop makes the decision not to call a student to become a priest, his action establishes that the young man did not truly have a vocation to the priesthood.

Young men must normally be at least 25 years old to become priests. Bishops have the authority to lower this age limit by one year, but only the Holy See can authorize the ordination of anyone younger than 24 years old.

*Below A deacon assists at the Mass. Transitional deacons become familiar with the priestly functions they will perform once they have completed their ordination.*

## TAKING VOWS

At ordination priests take vows of celibacy and of obedience to their bishop. Priests in religious orders take a vow of poverty in addition to those of obedience and celibacy. Before they can actively serve, priests have to be "incardinated" by a bishop or certain other religious superiors, such as the head of a religious order. This word derives from the Latin word for "a hinge", and when a priest is incardinated it means he is attached to and subject to a religious superior.

In practice, the priest will promise obedience to the bishop during his ordination service. However, if the priest has already made a vow of obedience to the superior of a religious order, then he will also acknowledge this pre-existing vow during his ordination.

*Above After a priest takes his vows of celibacy during his ordination, the bishop will practise laying on of hands – this is a symbolic gesture that has been used since the Old Testament.*

# MARRIED TO THE CHURCH

A PRIEST IS EXPECTED TO EMBRACE A CELIBATE LIFE. BEING CELIBATE ENABLES HIM TO AVOID WORLDLY DISTRACTIONS AND CONCENTRATE ON DEDICATING HIS LIFE TO SERVING GOD.

Roman Catholics believe that a priest's celibate life is a reflection of heaven. Priests are said to be married to the Church. The catechism declares that priests who embrace celibacy are "called to consecrate themselves with undivided heart to God…and give themselves entirely to God and to men" and that when it is accepted "with a joyous heart", "celibacy radiantly proclaims the Reign of God". Celibacy is a gift from the priest to God and to the people, to be made in a spirit of service.

The Church stresses that requiring celibacy in priests does not devalue the sacrament of marriage.

*Below Both brothers and sisters in Christ make sacrifices in adapting their lives to harmonize with the Church's teachings.*

Being a priest or entering married life are among the four vocations recognized by Catholics – and no one vocation is said to be superior to any of the others.

## BIBLICAL JUSTIFICATION

There is a principal source often cited by the Church in support of a call for clerical celibacy, a biblical passage found in Matthew, Chapter 19. In this passage Christ gives a description of marriage as a divinely ordained union between man and woman, and declares that any man who divorces his wife on grounds other than "unchastity" and then takes another is committing adultery. The disciples then say that if this is true it is surely better not to marry. In his response Christ apparently agrees, saying "Not all men can receive this saying, but only those to whom it is given" – that is, not everyone can accept this. He then adds, in the key verse (Matthew 19:12) that is generally cited by Roman Catholics:

> *For there are eunuchs who have been so from birth, and there are eunuchs who have been made eunuchs by men, and there are eunuchs who have made themselves eunuchs for the sake of the kingdom of heaven.*
> *He who is able to receive this, let him receive it.*

By the word that is translated as "eunuchs", Christ is thought to mean men who are celibate, who have freely chosen not to have sexual relations. Priests are an example of those in Christ's third category, who are celibate "for the sake of the kingdom of heaven".

*Above A priest consecrates himself to a new life and adopts celibacy, as stated in the catechism, "for the love of God's kingdom and the service of men".*

Another key biblical justification for the celibacy requirement can be found in the writing of St Paul in the First Letter to Corinthians (7:32-4): "The unmarried man is anxious about the affairs of the Lord, how to please the Lord; but the married man is anxious about worldly affairs, how to please his wife, and his interests are divided." These verses clearly support the Church's position that a celibate life frees a priest to concentrate on serving God and man.

## PRESSURE ON THE CHURCH

In the late 20th and early 21st centuries, critics inside and outside the Church have questioned the requirement of celibacy in priests. In an era of sexual liberation through much of Western society, the vow of celibacy has apparently made it more difficult to attract young men to the priesthood. There has been a mounting crisis in vocations, with the Church unable to replace priests who die and a number of parishes being left without priests.

## THE CHURCH HOLDS FIRM

Nevertheless, the requirement of sexual abstinence by priests has been repeatedly reaffirmed by the Church hierarchy. The Second Vatican Council's Decree on the Ministry and Life of Priests in 1965 addressed the issue and claimed that celibacy was a charitable act of the priest, one that provided "a source of spiritual fruitfulness in the world".

In 1967, Pope Paul VI expressed in his encyclical *On Priestly Celibacy* that when a priest dedicates himself to God through celibacy, he can form a more profound relation with God, and this would benefit humankind. The priest would be better prepared to devote himself to his parishioners. In 1979, Pope John Paul II declared in a letter to priests that in order to serve their fellow humans, the priests must be free in their hearts – and that celibacy is a sign of this freedom.

*Right Pope Paul VI called celibacy a special kind of asceticism that is more exacting than the sacrifices demanded of other Christians.*

*Below Pope Paul VI, enthroned, opens the Second Vatican Council in 1965. In its deliberations, the Council made notable pronouncements on celibacy.*

### MARRIED PRIESTS?

There are some exceptions to the strict requirement of celibacy. Certain Protestant ministers who are married and then convert to Catholicism are allowed to serve as priests while married if they are given authority by the pope. Men of mature age who are married may be ordained and serve as permanent deacons – that is, they may be deacons but may not become priests. Men who have been ordained deacons while single may not later marry.

# CALLED TO SERVE

IN THE SACRAMENT OF HOLY ORDERS, CANDIDATES ARE ORDAINED AS BISHOP, PRIEST OR DEACON. THE PROFOUND, BEAUTIFUL CEREMONIAL CONTAINS MOMENTS OF POWERFUL VISUAL THEATRE.

There are three types of ordination: as bishop, priest or deacon. On his ordination the candidate will join the relevant order – of bishops, priests or deacons. The word "ordination" means the incorporating of an individual into an order.

Only bishops have the power to perform ordinations. The essential rite of the sacrament is when the bishop lays his hands on the head of the candidate, or ordinand, and pronounces the prayer of consecration. It is traditional, but not required, for

**Above** *An ordinand puts his clasped hands between those of his bishop as a sign of faithfulness to his ecclesiastical superior.*

the ordination to take place during a Mass; ordinations are often held on a Sunday in the cathedral of the presiding bishop.

## THE ORDINAND'S EXAM

In the usual service of ordination, the ordinands are called forward to the altar after the reading of the gospel. The presentation follows, when the bishop asks a series of questions to establish that the candidates have passed through the necessary levels of training in their formation as priests and that they are worthy to become priests. The bishop then "elects" – that is, chooses – each candidate and offers the prayer: "We rely on the help of the Lord God and our Saviour Jesus Christ and we choose this man, our brother, for priesthood in the presbyteral order." The congregation present then signals its support by applauding.

**Left** *Prostrating himself while the bishop prays the Litany of the Saints, the ordinand shows his reliance on the Holy Spirit and the support of the faithful.*

The candidates sit while the bishop delivers a homily (sermon) on the nature of priesthood and the role of the priest. The candidates then come forward to the altar once more for the examination, in which the bishop asks whether they are willing: to discharge the office of the priesthood; to celebrate Christ's mysteries; to exercise the ministry of the Word; and to consecrate their lives to God through Christ the High Priest. They reply each time "I am".

## VOW OF OBEDIENCE

Each ordinand goes forward and, putting his hands in those of the bishop, promises to respect and be obedient to the bishop and his successors. (In some forms of the ordination service, when the candidates are being ordained as priests in a religious order, rather than as diocesan priests, they instead make a vow of obedience to the superior of the religious order to which they belong.) The bishop prays, "May God who has begun the good work in you bring it to fulfilment."

Next the ordinands lie prostrate on the floor while the bishop and assembled faithful recite the Litany of the Saints. The ordinands lie face down to symbolize their unworthiness to be a priest (or bishop or deacon, depending on the service) and the fact that to take on and succeed in the job they depend on the grace of God, and the prayers both of the saints and martyrs and of the Christian Community on Earth.

## LAYING ON OF HANDS

The ordinands kneel. The ordaining bishop places his hands on the head of each ordinand in silence. The already ordained priests helping at the service do likewise. The laying on

*Right The laying on of hands is a principal ritual that symbolizes the granting of priestly authority and the descent of the Holy Spirit.*

of hands is an ancient ritual going back to Old Testament times, when it was used by Jews to install their priests. The gesture is symbolic of the bishop's prayer to the Holy Spirit to descend on the candidate, and also of the long tradition of sacerdotal, or priestly, authority running right back to the time of the apostles.

The bishop says the Prayer of Consecration. He prays to the Holy Spirit to descend on the priest-to-be, to give him gifts needed for the ministry to which he is called.

## THE NEW PRIEST

Priests who are newly ordained now put on the stole and chasuble, the vestments worn by priests when celebrating Mass. The bishop anoints the hands of each new priest with chrism (consecrated oil), which is symbolic of Christ himself as High Priest. The newly made priests then wipe the chrism from their hands on cloths. (They usually give these to their mothers in recognition of the women's sacrifice in giving their sons to the service of the Church.)

The new priests are given patens and chalices that have been brought forward by the people. The bishop prays: "Accept from the holy people of God the gifts to be offered to Him.

*Above A newly ordained priest receives from the bishop the chalice and paten he will use to celebrate his first Mass.*

Know what you are doing, and imitate the mystery you celebrate: model your life on the mystery of the Lord's Cross."

The bishop makes the sign of peace to the newly ordained priests. They then join with the bishop in celebrating the Eucharist. At the close of the Mass service the bishop will kneel before the altar and the priests will give him their blessing. The priests can now share in Christ's own eternal priesthood: they have now been ordained to serve the Church as Christ did many centuries earlier.

# UNDER ORDERS

MEMBERS OF RELIGIOUS ORDERS UNDERTAKE TO FOLLOW A RELIGIOUS RULE OR WAY OF LIFE UNDER THE LEADERSHIP OF A SUPERIOR. THEY MAKE A FORMAL DEDICATION OF THEIR LIVES TO GOD.

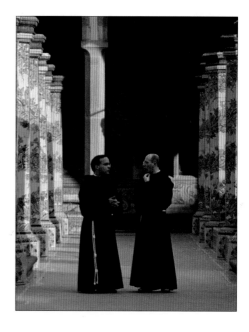

Religious orders are also known as Institutes of Consecrated Life. Their members take solemn public vows of chastity, poverty and obedience under Church law. Some members of religious orders are also ordained as priests or deacons, but if they are not they are considered to be members of the laity rather than clergy.

Within a religious order, authority is centralized in a superior or general house, which holds jurisdiction over geographically distributed dependent houses. However, a major exception to this general rule is the Order of St Benedict, in which there is no single superior house with overall authority and each of the individual abbeys is autonomous.

### THE RELIGIOUS ORDERS

Some members are known as monks and nuns, or simply monastics, and live in enclosed communities. They devote their lives primarily to prayer and devotions. Others are known as friars and religious sisters, or mendicants, and live in a more open context and engage in social, medical or educational work. Historically, the monastics are self-supporting, while the mendicant orders rely on alms for their upkeep.

There is also a distinction between canons regular and clerks regular. Those known as canons regular live in either a closed community or as secular canons in open society. Although they are first and foremost monks, some of them are priests. They devote themselves primarily to the monastic life, which is centred on celebration of the liturgy and on contemplation. Conversely, clerks regular are first and foremost priests, but they choose to live in a community following a religious rule, in a similar manner to monks. Clerks regular devote themselves primarily to the ministry of the priesthood.

### TAKING OF VOWS

Members of religious orders take what are known as solemn vows of obedience, chastity and poverty. Under solemn vows they renounce

*Above Franciscan friars confer in the cloisters of Santa Chiara in Naples, Italy. They share the complex with nuns of the Poor Clares.*

the right to own property. Members of another type of order, called religious congregations, take "simple" vows. In practice, those who swear simple vows retain the right to own material possessions, but they hand over the administration of the possessions to the congregation. Simple vows can be for a limited period, whereas solemn vows are for life. Those serving as novices, who are in the process of becoming a

---

### RULE OF LIFE

The "rule of life" is a set of guidelines that govern all aspects of behaviour by members of a religious order. Major examples in the Roman Catholic tradition include:

- The Rule of St Francis of Assisi, which is followed by those in the Franciscan tradition, such as the Order of the Friars Minor
- The Rule of St Benedict, followed by the Benedictines
- The Rule of St Augustine, which is traditionally followed by the Augustinians.

*Right Benedictine monks harvest flowers in the grounds of the 11th-century Abbey of Santa Maria Assunta at Praglia, near Padua, Italy.*

*Above Jesuits are led from Rome by the Superior General, who holds the office for life. Spanish father Adolfo Nicolas was appointed in 2008.*

monk or nun, swear simple vows for a limited period before professing solemn vows for life.

There is another kind of religious community in which members do not take any vows. This is called a Society of Apostolic Life. A bishop grants this kind of society authority to operate in his diocese. An example is the Catholic Foreign Missionary Society of America.

## SOCIETY OF JESUS

Jesuits are an important example of clerks regular. They are members of the Society of Jesus, which was established in the 1530s by Spaniard Ignatius Loyola in Paris. Today the society is governed from its head-quarters in Rome, the General Curia, by the Superior General (also known as Father General), who is confirmed in his position by the pope. The Father General is assisted by an advisory council in Rome;

around the world, the order is split into geographic provinces, each one led by a Father Superior.

The Society is the largest religious order of priests in the Catholic Church. About 13,500 of its 20,000 members are priests, with around 1,800 brothers, 3,000 students and almost 1,000 novices. From its early days the society combined strong central authority with mobility. Jesuits place emphasis on obedience to the pope – they are said to take a "fourth vow" (in addition to those of poverty, obedience and chastity) of particular obedience to the pope. Because Loyola had a military background, and due to this particular reverence for the papacy's authority, the Jesuits are sometimes referred to as the "Foot soldiers of the pope".

*Right A statue of Father John Carroll sits in front of the Jesuit university of Georgetown. He founded the private university in 1789.*

## JESUIT EDUCATION

Priests and brothers engage in many kinds of evangelical work, including missions and social work in less developed countries, but they are associated with education. Their first university, the Pontifical Gregorian University, or Gregorianum, in Rome, has been providing education since its foundation in 1551.

The Jesuits staff and run many schools, colleges, seminaries, universities and theological colleges. They work in more than 112 different countries around the world, and their education work is particularly important in India and the United States. In India, the Jesuits maintain colleges and schools in Mumbai, Calcutta, Delhi and Goa. In the United States, the Jesuits run more than 50 universities, colleges and schools, including the celebrated Georgetown University, which was founded in Washington, D.C., and Fordham University, which is located in New York City.

# BROTHERS IN CHRIST

ONE BRANCH OF THE RELIGIOUS ORDERS STRESSES THE SPIRITUAL BENEFITS OF COMMUNITY LIVING. MONKS FOLLOW A RELIGIOUS RULE CENTRED ON CELEBRATING THE LITURGY OF THE HOURS TOGETHER.

St Benedict of Nursia, author of the *Rule of St Benedict*, is often celebrated as being the founder of Western monasticism. Modern Benedictines are the successors of the 6th-century monks for whom Benedict, founder of the monastery at Monte Cassino in Italy, wrote his rule of life in *c.* AD 535–40.

In a prologue and 73 chapters, the *Rule of St Benedict* directs monks to divide their time mainly between common prayer, prayerful meditative reading and manual work. The monks are expected to work six hours a day with their hands. The Rule, which St Benedict calls "a school of the Lord's service", also gives detailed guidance on acceptable sleeping arrangements, food and drink, clothing and caring for the sick, as well as hospitality for guests and recruitment. Although

*Below The brothers of Bec Abbey at Le Bec-Hellouin, a Benedictine abbey in France, are joined for Mass by the sisters of the nearby Monastère de Ste Françoise Romaine.*

modern Benedictines do not follow the rule so strictly, they do still use it to guide their lives.

## THE ORGANIZATION

From early on the Benedictines were organized to allow for local decision-making. Each monastery or "house" is autonomous, and the houses are grouped in 21 congregations. In 1893, Pope Leo XIII established the Benedictine Confederation of the Order of St Benedict, which is a confederation of the autonomous congregations, and appointed an abbot primate as its head. The abbot primate does not have direct jurisdiction in Benedictine monasteries but has a general concern for the wellbeing of Benedictines worldwide. The headquarters of the confederation is in Rome.

## A LIFE GOVERNED BY VOWS

Benedictine monks take three vows: of obedience, that they promise to live according to the Rule of St Benedict; of stability, that they will endeavour to remain in the

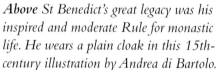

*Above St Benedict's great legacy was his inspired and moderate Rule for monastic life. He wears a plain cloak in this 15th-century illustration by Andrea di Bartolo.*

Benedictine order for life; and of conversion, that they will seek to follow Christ's example in all things, and will transform their life by adopting poverty and chastity.

In a typical Benedictine house, the monk's day is structured around six church services in the Liturgy of the Hours, with intervening periods of work and private prayer with meditative reading (known as *lectio divina*). The typical day includes four hours in liturgical prayer, five hours in private prayer and spiritual reading, six hours of labour and eight hours of sleep. The remaining hour is set aside for eating.

A monk is required to attend the liturgical services. The first service is the "night office" of matins, which is prayed while still dark, and this is followed by the "morning office" of lauds at dawn. The monks work in the morning, and meet for midday prayer. They then work again in the afternoon, and celebrate Mass together in the late afternoon. The evening services are vespers (evening prayer) and compline (night prayer), which is said and sung before the monks retire to sleep.

The monks view their times of prayer and reading as their true work, but they are also required by the Rule of St Benedict to work. It warns that idleness can be dangerous to the life of the soul and urges brothers to keep themselves busy, sometimes at manual labour and at other times, in spiritual reading. The Rule specifically calls on the monks to work with their hands, but in modern monasteries the work done varies according to circumstance. Many Benedictine houses run schools in which monks work as teachers and administrators; there is also a good deal of practical work in and around the monastery: in the gardens, kitchens and laundry. In some houses, the monks also run a parish and keep a retreat house. They also often perform social work with local people.

## BECOMING A MONK

A young man who wants to become a monk typically starts by staying in the monastery for a period as a visitor, then progresses to being a

*Right The Rule of St Benedict encourages brothers to work with their hands each day. A monk works prayerfully in his pottery studio.*

postulant. As a postulant he commits to living in the monastery alongside the monks for three to six months.

He may leave after six months, or commit to being a novice. As a novice he is "clothed": this means he is given his monk's habit or cloak. After one or two years as a novice, the young man may be asked to renew his simple (temporary) vows for three years. After three years he may take solemn (life) vows and become

*Above Brothers share a meal. Their communal life is known as cenobitic monasticism, from the ancient Greek words* koinos *and* bios *("common" and "life").*

a monk. He can continue as a novice for six or nine years, but after that period he must take life vows or leave the monastery. At any point when the applicant is free to leave, he may also be asked to leave if the abbot thinks he is not suited to monastic life.

## DECLINING NUMBERS

Membership of the Roman Catholic Church is on the rise, but the number of those living a monastic life is in decline. Figures released in February 2008 showed that the number of members of the consecrated life fell a little under 10 per cent in 2005–6 to 945,210. There are many more nuns and sisters than brothers and friars. Of those in the consecrated life, around 750,000 are women compared to approximately 190,000 men. Today, around 8,400 men and 14,600 women live in monastic communities. They follow different rules of life.

# A CONTEMPLATIVE CHRISTIANITY

IN THE TRADITION OF CONTEMPLATIVE MONASTICISM, MONKS LIVE IN AN ENCLOSED COMMUNITY AND COMMIT TO A LIFE OF SELF–DISCIPLINE AND PRAYER ON BEHALF OF THE CHURCH AND THE WORLD.

*Above St Bruno was a brilliant theologian and teacher. In this detail from a 17th-century painting by Nicholas Regnier, he is receiving the order.*

Contemplative monks have no active ministry in terms of pastoral or missionary work or charitable enterprises, and they have little social interaction except through prayer. They generally live under strict rules governing their interaction. They spend large parts of the day alone and endeavour to live largely in silence. They usually work to produce goods by which they wholly or partially support themselves.

Members of the Carthusian Order (or the Order of St Bruno) live a life of this kind. The order was founded by St Bruno of Cologne in 1084 and takes its name from Chartreuse in France, where Bruno established his first hermitage with six companions. Carthusian monasteries are headed by a prior. They contain a community of cloister

*Below The mother house of the Carthusian Order is the remote monastery of La Grande Chartreuse, which is based in the Chartreuse Mountains of eastern France.*

monks (sometimes called fathers), who commit to greater solitude, and brothers (or lay brothers), who have a less solitary life and take on the material tasks necessary to the running of the house.

In England, Carthusian monasteries are called charterhouses. The order is open to women as well as to men. There are currently 24 charterhouses worldwide – 19 monasteries, holding 370 monks, and 5 nunneries, holding 75 nuns.

## LIFE IN A HERMITAGE

In a typical charterhouse, each of the cloister monks has his own hermitage, or living quarters, which usually has two storeys. Below is a workshop and wood for the wood-burning stove that is the hermitage's source of heat. The main room, above, is the cubiculum. The hermitage also has its own water supply and lavatory.

In the cubiculum, the monk prays, studies, sleeps and eats. He follows most of the Liturgy of the Hours, using full ceremony as if in public, although three daily services are celebrated communally in the chapel attached to the monastery. The monk enters the cubiculum through a small antechamber, which is known as the Ave Maria. This symbolizes the fact that in prayer the monk comes to Christ by way of the Blessed Virgin Mary. He begins all his offices and other prayers with intercessions to the Virgin. In the workshop area, the monk performs work for at least two hours a day.

The hermitage adjoins a walled garden in which the cloister monk meditates and grows vegetables and flowers. Each of the hermitages gives

on to a communal cloister through a turnstile: food and other materials can be left in this area without disturbing the cloister monk, which allows the contemplative monk to maintain absolute solitude.

Unlike the monks, the brothers of the community spend less time in prayer and more maintaining the monastery. They are responsible for managing food and other supplies, preparing meals, organizing the library and delivering books to cloister monks, carrying out repairs around the charterhouse and so on.

## SILENCE

The monks attempt to live in silence. Although they do not take a vow of silence, they try to speak only when strictly necessary. They aim by this discipline to cultivate inner serenity.

Each cloister monk leaves his hermitage three times a day for services in the main chapel. These are the night offices (matins), the morning Eucharist and vespers in the evening. Occasionally, he meets his superior for a conference. On feast days and Sundays, all the monks meet for a community meal, held in silence. Once a week the brothers participate in a four-hour walk in the countryside around the charterhouse. They are permitted to speak on the walk: they walk in pairs, and change partners every 30 minutes. Two times a year the monks join in a

*Above A documentary film* Into Great Silence *(2005) provided an insight into the lives of Carthusian monks at La Grande Chartreuse.*

community day of recreation and once annually they receive a visit from family.

## THE SOLITARY LIFE

The Carthusian motto is the Latin *Stat crux dum volvitur orbis* ("The Cross holds steady while the world turns"). It celebrates the idea that silent contemplation and solitary prayer can create a place of sacred stillness amid change. The place of stillness serves to sanctify the wider world.

The monks endeavour to interiorize the silence amid which they live. They report that by a spiritual paradox, in solitude they can experience unity with all God's Creation. Through this experience their hearts are expanded to the dimensions of the love felt by Christ himself, for all people and all creatures.

The Carthusians live by a rule known as the Statutes. It declares that the hermitage is on holy ground and is a place where the monks can talk to God, where "earth meets heaven, and the divine meets the human". Carthusians aim to live in a state of constant and pure prayer, to exist in the presence of God and to maintain their hearts as an altar from which prayer rises constantly to God.

*Above A monk at La Trappe Abbey in Normandy, France, reads in front of a 1692 portrait of Father de Rancé, who was the founder of the Trappists.*

# WORKING IN THE WORLD

ANOTHER BRANCH OF THE RELIGIOUS ORDERS, KNOWN AS THE MENDICANTS, MAKES IT A PRIORITY TO PREACH THE WORD OF GOD AND TO PERFORM GOOD WORKS IN SOCIETY.

The mendicant orders are distinct from the monastic orders. The calling of monastic orders, such as the Benedictines or the Carthusians, is to live a life of self-disciplined routine and devotion in a monastery. While many monastic orders minister to the world through schools, parishes and retreat houses attached to their monasteries, the mendicant orders follow a call to engage directly with the wider world. They traditionally rely on the charity of others for support as they administer their work.

The mendicant orders also have a different organization. Brothers are attached to a province rather than to an individual monastery. They are answerable to a provincial superior general instead of to the abbot or prior of their own religious house.

Brothers and priests in the mendicant orders are known as friars, which distinguishes them from their counterparts in the monastic orders, who are called monks. "Friar" comes from the French *frère* and the Latin *frater* (both meaning "brother").

## THE FOUR GREAT ORDERS

Of the mendicant orders, four of them in particular are referred to as the "great orders": the Franciscans, the Dominicans, the Carmelites and the Augustinians. They were recognized as the four Great Orders at the Second Council of Lyon (the Fourteenth Ecumenical Council of the Roman Catholic Church) in 1274. There are other mendicant orders, which are generally known as the lesser mendicant orders (*see Catholic Mendicant Orders, left*).

The Franciscans were founded in about 1209 by St Francis of Assisi. They are sometimes called the Friars

*Above Franciscan friars gather to follow the Via Dolorosa ("Way of Grief") in Jerusalem on Good Friday. Devotions are the ground from which good works grow.*

Minor because Francis called his followers *fratres minores* ("lesser brothers") to place stress on their humility. They are traditionally called the Grey Friars because they wear a grey habit. The Dominicans were established in around 1215 by St Dominic; they are often called the Black Friars because they wear a

*Below A Carmelite friar from Aylesford Priory in Kent, England, leads local children in learning and worship. The priory was founded in the 13th century.*

## CATHOLIC MENDICANT ORDERS

The great and lesser mendicant orders are listed below, with the year they were established:
- Franciscans, founded in 1209
- Dominicans, founded *c.*1214
- Carmelites, founded *c.*1155, mendicant order from 1245
- Augustinians, founded in 1256
- Minims, founded in 1474
- Conventual Franciscans, founded in 1517
- Capuchins, founded in 1520
- Third Order Regular of St Francis, founded in 1521
- Discalced Carmelites, founded in 1568
- Discalced Trinitarians, founded in 1593
- Order of Penance, founded in 1781

*Right Children orphaned by the tsunami disaster of 2004 can attend a new nursery that has been set up by the Salesians of Don Bosco in Sri Lanka.*

black *cappa*, or "cloak", over a white habit. The Carmelites were founded in about 1155, originally as a contemplative order, but they became mendicants in 1245. They are also called the White Friars because they wear a white cloak over a brown habit. In 1255, the Augustinians were founded as a mendicant order from various groups of hermits by Pope Alexander IV and follow a rule based on the writings of St Augustine. They wear black garments too.

## THE FRIARS' WORK

Many thousands of friars in the mendicant orders engage with needs across the world. Augustinian friars work as teachers, missionaries and also as parish priests; there are more than 2,700 Augustinian friars serving in about 40 countries. Franciscan friars work in virtually every country in the world. They have a special calling to work with the poor, in shelters, hospitals, schools and in programmes supporting justice and peace.

Dominican friars have a special calling to preach the gospel – indeed their official title is the Order of Preachers. They are also strongly committed to communal religious life, which they see as an essential support for their preaching work. According to their constitutions, they commit themselves to study assiduously, to celebrate the liturgy and especially the Eucharist together, to persevere and "to live with one mind the common life".

Dominican friars live in priories under an elected prior, where they sing the Mass and Holy Liturgy

*Right Street children from Nairobi enjoy working the land at a youth centre founded in 1994 by the Salesians of Don Bosco in Langata, Kenya.*

together and share their meals and times of recreation. They commit to spreading the gospel wherever their work takes them, whether it is in hospitals, prisons, universities or schools. They see publishing books and dissemination of the gospel on the Internet as part of their work. These friars aim to emulate their

founder, of whom it was said that he was always either talking to God or about God.

## TEACHING ORDERS

Some religious orders are devoted particularly to teaching in schools and colleges. The De La Salle brothers, which was founded in 17th-century France by St Jean-Baptiste de La Salle, a canon at Rheims Cathedral, runs schools in 80 countries teaching more than 900,000 students.

The Salesians of Don Bosco, which was founded in 19th-century Italy by St John Bosco, are committed to working with young people in need. The Salesians number more than 16,000 priests and brothers who work with the young in 128 countries.

The Salesians run a large number of secondary or high schools, including: in London, Farnborough and Bolton in England; in Los Angeles and Richmond, California, and New Rochelle, New York, in the United States; at Imphal and Calcutta in India; and one in Hong Kong. They also run college-level educational establishments, which include DeSales University in Pennsylvania.

# BRIDES OF CHRIST

WOMEN ENTER RELIGIOUS ORDERS TO SERVE GOD THROUGH PRAYER, DEVOTIONS AND GOOD WORKS. WOMEN CALLED TO RELIGIOUS SERVICE ARE CALLED "BRIDES OF CHRIST".

When women commit themselves to religious life they can choose to become nuns or religious sisters. The words "nun" and "sister" are often not distinguished in common usage, but strictly speaking a nun is a woman who has taken vows, committing herself to an enclosed life of prayer and contemplative devotions within a convent, while a religious sister has chosen a much more actively engaged life of service, caring for the sick, starving, poor and otherwise needy.

## LIFE IN A CONVENT

Nuns live in a monastery or a convent. A monastery is normally thought to be a community of monks

*Below Sisters of contemplative orders work tirelessly and devotedly through prayer to bring peace and God's love to a troubled world.*

and a convent to be a community of nuns, but some communities of monks are also called convents and some communities of nuns are referred to as monasteries, especially in the Benedictine tradition. (Religious communities of nuns were once also called nunneries, but this word is now archaic.)

Nuns live an enclosed life. They are not generally permitted to leave the convent or to receive visitors, although some do carry out teaching or other ministries as permitted by the constitution or rule of their particular community. Strictly, convents should be built so that the inner courtyards and gardens cannot be seen from without and the windows do not open on to public roads.

The convents are independent of one another, with each community headed by a Mother Superior. She is usually elected for life, but

*Above Today's nuns still follow the advice of the 16th-century nun St Teresa of Ávila, who taught sisters that Christ "has no hands on earth but yours".*

in some constitutions the Mother Superior is subject to re-election every three years.

If the community is an abbey, she is known as an abbess, and if it is a priory she is a prioress. The distinction made between abbey and priory depends on differences in the particular religious orders and in the community's level of independence.

## STEPS TO SISTERHOOD

If a young woman feels she has a calling to the religious life as a nun or sister, she becomes a postulant for six months to a year. During this time she usually lives in the community, following the life of the nuns and sisters closely, but takes no vows. If she and the order then determine that she has a vocation, she is generally given the habit (clothing) of the order and lives for one to two years as a novice; at this point she still takes no vows. The next stage is to take temporary vows for one year or

*Right Work is a form of prayer for nuns, such as for these English Benedictine sisters attentively labouring over the ironing.*

more, up to six years. The last stage is to take final vows and make perpetual profession.

The vows the nuns take will vary from one order to another. In the Benedictine tradition nuns, such as Trappistines and Cistercians, take a threefold vow of stability (to remain a member of the community), of obedience to the Mother Superior and of conversion of life (to adopt poverty and chastity). Franciscan and Dominican nuns take a vow of poverty, chastity and obedience. Some nuns take an extra vow specific to the kind of work they do or the character of their order.

## TYPES OF ORDERS

There are contemplative orders and charitable orders. Most of the strictly enclosed congregations of nuns are members of contemplative religious orders who are devoted to seeking union with God through prayer and contemplation. The Carmelite nuns, the Redemptoristines and the Poor Clares (or Order of Poor Ladies) are all examples of contemplative orders. They sometimes undertake enclosed ministries by supporting a particular type of work through prayer in the convent: for example, the Redemptoristines pray for the work of the Redemptorist friars. They often support themselves by labour in the convent – for example, by making liturgical items, such as church candles and vestments.

Women in the charitable orders are committed to performing works of charity and mercy, teaching and caring for the sick or aged. Examples include the Little Sisters of the Poor, Ursulines and the Sisters of Charity.

### THE DEVOTION OF ST THÉRÈSE

St Thérèse of Lisieux was a French Carmelite nun of the late 19th century whose spiritual autobiography, *L'histoire d'une âme* ("Story of a Soul"), published in 1898, inspired great popular devotion. She was canonized in 1925 by Pope Pius XI and in 1997 Pope John Paul II declared her a Doctor of the Universal Church. She is one of three women among the 33 Doctors of the Church.

Thérèse, who is today popularly known as "the Little Flower of Jesus", became a Carmelite novice in April 1888 at the tender age of 15, following her sisters Pauline and Marie into the order. She died of tuberculosis on 30 September 1897 when just 24 years old. Thérèse is celebrated for her "Little Way" of devotion and love, which promotes the need for trust and absolute surrender. She wrote:

*Love shows itself in deeds....Great deeds are beyond me. The only way I can show my love is by throwing out flowers and these flowers are each a small sacrifice, each look and word, and doing of the very least thing simply for love.*

*Right St Thérèse was a teenage novice when she posed for this picture at the Carmelite house in Lisieux, c.1890.*

# LIVING FOR OTHERS

WOMEN IN THE RELIGIOUS ORDERS DEDICATE THEIR LIVES TO GOD IN CHRIST AND TO PRAYING FOR AND SERVING THOSE IN NEED BECAUSE OF POVERTY, SICKNESS OR IGNORANCE OF THE GOSPEL.

Whether nuns or religious sisters are members of a contemplative or charitable order, their religious life is intended to reach out to help other people. Enclosed orders seek to ease suffering in the world through devoted prayer, while charitable orders provide care, shelter, education and love to the needy.

### IN AN ENCLOSED ORDER
The Poor Clares, which was established in 1212 by St Clare of Assisi and St Francis of Assisi, is an enclosed contemplative order of Franciscan nuns who are committed to a life of prayer without possessions. These nuns pray the Holy Liturgy and

*Below Sisters in the Poor Clares dedicate themselves to service through prayer. Some undertake strict acts of penance, fasts and other austerities.*

celebrate Mass together. They see intercessionary prayer as an important part of their calling, and they accept prayer requests from outside the convent and pray daily for the Church and the world.

Some houses keep retreat centres in the grounds of the convent. They also work in their convent to maintain the community as well as to support themselves. To this aim, they might make candles, vestments, greeting cards or religious pictures. The nuns follow a rota for cooking, gardening, cleaning, answering calls and so on.

The nuns view the enclosed life they live as a vital spiritual discipline that expresses their love for God. They leave the enclosed community only when it is absolutely necessary – perhaps to visit the doctor or dentist or to see a parent who cannot

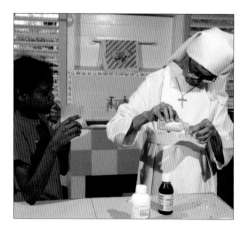

*Above A sister distributes medicine at an Ursuline orphanage in Guyana, South America. The Ursulines have a special calling to education and healthcare.*

travel. They are permitted to receive visits by close family members as allowed by the abbess.

### CARING FOR THE POOR
Among many orders of nuns dedicated to charitable work in the world, the Missionaries of Charity, a religious order with a special calling to serve the extremely poor, is one of the most celebrated in modern times. The order was established in 1950 by Mother Teresa of Calcutta, and today it includes 4,500 nuns working in 133 countries.

These nuns care for orphans, lepers, victims of AIDS, refugees, former prostitutes, street children, the mentally ill and those suffering in the wake of famine and natural disasters. In Calcutta, the place of their foundation, they maintain no fewer than 19 homes, including ones for the dying, for lepers and a school for street children. The nuns in this order take the conventional vows of poverty, chastity and obedience. They also take a fourth vow to offer "wholehearted and free service to the poorest of the poor".

### CARING FOR THE OLD
The Little Sisters of the Poor is a religious order with a particular calling to care for the elderly. The order

## MOTHER TERESA

Albanian Agnes Gonxha Bojaxhiu (later Mother Teresa) was a Roman Catholic nun who went to India as a missionary and took her solemn vows in 1937. She reported that she received a call from God to work with the poor in Calcutta in 1946, and in 1950 she received permission from the Vatican to establish the Diocesan Congregation of the Calcutta Diocese, which became the Missionaries of Charity. She opened her first home for the dying in Calcutta in 1952. In the 1960s, the order expanded through India and around the world. In the 1970s, she was internationally recognized for her work and received the Nobel Peace Prize in 1979. She died on 5 September 1997 and was beatified by Pope John Paul II in 2003 under the name Blessed Teresa of Calcutta.

*Right* Mother Teresa declared that her mission was to care for the hungry, destitute and those without homes, for all people who feel that others do not want or love them.

was established in 1839 in France by Jeanne Jugan, but they have a strong presence in many cities in the United States. Today the order has approximately 4,000 sisters caring for more than 22,000 elderly people in 34 countries, including India, Hong Kong, Taiwan and the United Kingdom. In the United States alone, the Little Sisters of the Poor are responsible for running 32 homes for the elderly, including houses in San Francisco, Washington, D.C., New Orleans, Indianapolis and Pittsburgh.

The Little Sisters of the Poor put into practice their founder's instuctions to always show kindness toward others, but particularly to those who are sick. Jeanne Jugan had stressed that the calling to serve the sick was a great sign of God's Grace, and she declared that because the infirm were God's creatures, when the sisters cared for the sick they were serving God himself.

The nuns rely on charitable contributions to support their work, and they generally tour the area around their home in a "begging van", in which they collect gifts not only of food but also of medical and other important supplies.

*Right* The Benedictine sisters in this early 18th-century French painting by Louise Madeleine care for the sick.

In addition to vows of obedience, chastity and poverty, the sisters take a fourth vow of hospitality. They endeavour not just to give their residents shelter, food and comfort, but also to cater for their spiritual, psychological and social needs.

### PRAYER AND DEVOTION

Sisters in charitable orders, such as the Missionaries of Charity and the Little Sisters of the Poor, anchor their active life in a routine of prayer and contemplative devotions. The Little Sisters of the Poor, for instance, will typically start the day with meditation and morning prayer, and then hold a daily Mass at the end of the morning. Residents in their homes are welcomed to this service. The sisters also take time for regular prayer throughout the day and they engage in meditative religious reading, or *lectio divina*. In addition, they meet for evening prayer at the end of the day.

# THE MISSIONS

A NUMBER OF ROMAN CATHOLIC RELIGIOUS ORDERS ARE DEDICATED TO MISSIONARY WORK. THEY WORK ACROSS THE WORLD IN BOTH DEVELOPED AND DEVELOPING COUNTRIES TO SPREAD THE GOSPEL.

There are many Catholic missionary orders, but the Missionaries of the Sacred Heart, an order founded in France in 1854 by French priest Jules Chevalier, is particularly notable.

### WORLDWIDE MISSION
The Sacred Heart has about 2,000 brothers and priests working around the world in more than 50 countries from Australia to Venezuela, inspired by their founder to find opportunities to serve Christ in the depths of the world's need. Chevalier was convinced that Christians could have as profound an experience of God's

*Below The brothers of some missionaries are active in helping the poverty-stricken, such as these from the Missionaries of the Poor, repairing roofs in Kingston, Jamaica.*

Grace in the world as they would in an enclosed religious community, and he declared that when brothers were helping the poor, the great power of God's love and of the Sacred Heart of Jesus would flow forth as needed. The greater the difficulties the brothers encountered in doing God's work, the greater the help God would provide.

Brothers still work in Papua New Guinea, where the order sent its first missionaries in 1882. They run the St Joseph Training Centre at Fissoa on the island of New Ireland, in which young men, many the sons of subsistence farmers from rural villages, study mathematics, English, music and religion while majoring in mechanics or carpentry. The young men also learn agricultural skills.

*Above The Sacred Heart of Jesus provides spiritual inspiration to the brothers of the Missionaries of the Sacred Heart.*

Many are given scholarships, paid from a fund set up by two of the Sacred Heart brothers.

The brothers, who are sometimes better known as MSC from the initials of their name in Latin, *Missionarii Sacratissimi Cordis*, declare that they see their work as "to be on Earth the heart of God", to meet need in whatever form they encounter it. In missions in England, Wales and Ireland, for example, they work with migrants and refugees in ecumenical interfaith initiatives and widely in education and parishes. Their motto is: "May the Sacred Heart of Jesus be everywhere loved."

On 1 September 2004, Pope John Paul II wrote to the Sacred Heart to mark its 150th anniversary, praising its founder and its work. He said that the organization's founder, Father Chevalier, established the Sacred Heart as a place for God to meet humankind, and expressed his wish that the community continue to inspire and have strength for its spiritual work. He also declared that they had a wonderful history worth remembering, but also "a great history still to be accomplished".

*Right A priest from the Catholic Foreign Missionary Society of America (Maryknoll) greets those attending a wedding Mass in Kibera, Nairobi, Kenya.*

## MARYKNOLL

Formerly known as the Catholic Foreign Missionary Society of America, Maryknoll sends more than 550 priests and brothers to work around the world, especially in Africa, Latin America, Korea, Japan and China. The order was founded in 1911 in the United States by Fathers James Anthony Walsh and Thomas Frederick Price.

In their mission statement, the brothers declare that, wherever they have travelled, they have been touched by the strength of human perseverance and greatly empowered by their experience of Christian faith in times of need. They work with them in declaring their faith in Jesus. The Maryknoll brothers commit themselves to standing in solidarity with the poor, to entering inter-religious dialogue, to serving as witnesses of Christ, to celebrating the Church's liturgy and to proclaiming the gospel and teaching the faith.

The society is linked to the Maryknoll Sisters of St Dominic, a group of religious sisters founded in 1912, in the United States. More than 700 Maryknoll Sisters work in 30 countries, including Albania, Panama, Nepal, Sudan and Taiwan. The sisters are associated with setting up convent schools. Widely known examples are Maryknoll Convent School in Kowloon Tong, Hong Kong, and Miriam College in Quezon City, Manila, the Philippines.

## OTHER MISSIONS

The larger religious orders, while not formed primarily to carry out missionary outreach, do a great deal of work of this kind. Among many examples, Capuchin Franciscans maintain missions in Central America (Panama and Nicaragua) and in South Africa. In Pretoria, South Africa, for example, they run the Damietta Peacemaking Initiative to promote non-violence and peace, from Padre Pio Friary in Rietvallei.

The Jesuits spread the gospel through their outreach work in educational establishments, orphanages, hospitals and community centres as part of their overseas missions – notably in Guyana, Zimbabwe and South Africa. The Carmelites also maintain several missions, including ones in Kenya, Mozambique, Indonesia, East Timor, Burkina Faso, Cameroon and the Democratic Republic of Congo. In Kenya, for instance, the Carmelites have established an enclosed monastery in Machakos and a house of formation in Ngong diocese.

Another notable order is the Missionaries of La Salette, which was founded in 1852 in La Salette, near Grenoble, France, where a shrine to the Blessed Virgin Mary was established. The order has around 1,000 nuns, priests and lay members working in support of healing and reconciliation in North America and Europe, as well as performing missionary work in countries such as Madagascar, the Philippines, Bolivia, Myanmar, Namibia and Angola.

*Right Franciscan sisters demonstrate God's love for the helpless by running an orphanage school in northern Egypt.*

# LAY GROUPS

THE CHURCH ENDORSES THE WORK OF SEVERAL ORGANIZATIONS THAT WERE ESTABLISHED TO HELP LAY CATHOLICS FOLLOW THE GOSPEL IN THEIR RELIGIOUS WORK AND FAMILY LIVES.

The largest lay group, Opus Dei (Latin for "God's work") is a Roman Catholic organization of predominately lay people who seek to grow closer to God and achieve sanctity through work and everyday activities, including family life. There are around 87,000 members worldwide, in 80 countries; 98 per cent are lay people and just 2 per cent priests. Approximately 30 per cent of lay members (called numeraries) are celibate and live in Opus Dei centres, while roughly 70 per cent (called supernumeraries) are married and serve God in family life.

The movement was founded in 1928 in Spain by Roman Catholic priest Josemaría Escrivá and received approval in 1950 from Pope Pius XII.

In 1982, Pope John Paul II declared the organization a personal prelature within the Church, under the name the Prelature of the Holy Cross and Opus Dei. This means that it functions like a religious order. The Church governs Opus Dei members through a prelate, who is appointed by the pope, and has a status equivalent to that of a superior general in a religious order. The members remain part of local church congregations.

As an organization, Opus Dei runs high schools, colleges, university halls of residence, business and agricultural schools, and it also does charitable work. In Spain, it founded and runs the University of Navarre at Pamplona. It also runs a university at Piura in Peru.

*Above* Pope John XXIII stands between St Josemaría Escrivá and Msgr Álvaro del Portillo, another leading Opus Dei figure, in 1960.

## A SECULAR ROUTINE

Josemaría Escrivá encouraged people to try to "convert their work into prayer". He described a dream in which God's children could sanctify themselves although they lived as ordinary citizens. It was through regular work and the mundane routine of everyday life that people could find God's love.

Escrivá died in 1975. Pope John Paul II beatified him in 1992 and proclaimed him a saint in 2002. John Paul II declared Escrivá the "saint of ordinary life", adding that he disseminated through society the awareness that a calling to holiness is received by all, with no distinctions of culture, racial identity, social class or age.

## SPIRITUALITY

Opus Dei members are expected to follow a set form of personal devotions every day, including Mass, and to attend a weekly confession. They should also attend an annual spiritual retreat of three weeks for numeraries and one week for supernumeraries.

*Left* The Church of Our Lady of Peace in Rome is the headquarters of Opus Dei. Many pray at the crypt of St Josemaría Escrivá.

Spiritual practice for a member of Opus Dei often includes an element of sacrifice by voluntarily offering discomfort or pain to God. This can simply involve self-sacrifice in terms of self-denial and charity in dealing with others. However, some celibate numeraries are said to practise physical mortification by either wearing a spike metal chain known as a cilice on the upper thigh or by flailing themselves with a woven cotton strap known as a discipline.

## A CRITICIZED PRACTICE

Self-mortification is one of many areas in which Opus Dei has been criticized. Opponents attack the practice as being akin to masochism and even liable to undermine spiritual development by fostering

---

### IN RECOGNITION FOR CHRISTIAN SERVICE

The Association of Papal Orders is an organization for people who have been awarded papal knighthoods. These awards are made at five levels to people who have provided a great service to the Catholic Church. The five levels are:
• Supreme Order of Christ
• Pontifical Order of the Golden Spur
• Pontifical Order of Pius IX
• Pontifical Order of St Gregory the Great
• Pontifical Order of Pope St Sylvester.

Notable recipients of the awards include Prince Rainier III of Monaco (Pontifical Order of the Golden Spur), former German Federal Chancellor Helmut Kohl (Pontifical Order of St Gregory the Great) and the Hollywood entertainer Bob Hope (Pontifical Order of Pope St Sylvester).

---

*Above A statue of St Josemaría Escrivá, founder of Opus Dei, stands in an alcove of the basilica façade within the Vatican.*

pride. However, defenders of the practice respond that it is a valued way of identifying with Christ's physical suffering, has been used by Christians for centuries and is more used today in the Roman Catholic Church than is generally known.

## A SECRETIVE SOCIETY

Opus Dei has been accused by some of being both secretive and manipulative. They claim that a number of leading politicians around the world are members of the society, although few make public statement of their membership. Some people suggest that the organization dominates members and uses overly aggressive recruitment techniques. Opus Dei, however, states that members are not coerced into joining and people are free to leave if they want to.

## OTHER LAY GROUPS

Many of the major religious orders also support lay associates: for example, the Dominican laity have their own rule, the Rule of the Lay Fraternities of St Dominic, first issued in 1285, while Franciscan lay

---

followers are members of the Secular Franciscan Order and follow a rule established for secular followers by St Francis himself in 1221. Secular Franciscans have a novitiate and formal profession, but they are not bound by their religious vows, and can be married and live ordinary lives in the community.

Among the other Catholic lay bodies is the Catenian Association, which is an international brotherhood of Catholic professionals and businessmen. It was established in 1908 in Manchester, England, and now has about 10,000 members in Australia, Ireland, South Africa, Malta, Zimbabwe and Zambia, as well as in the United Kingdom.

Their aims are to develop social bonds and foster brotherly love among members. The association grants bursaries to provide partial support for young Catholics who are performing community work. The Catenians also maintain a Public Affairs Committee that monitors and speaks out on any proposed legislation that would contradict Catholic teaching.

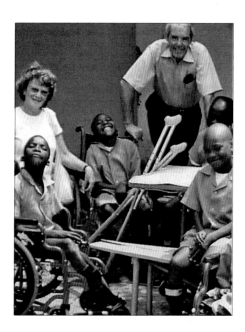

*Above The Catenian Association has sponsored projects to help the needy in Mexico and Africa, such as at this children's home in Zambia.*

# LIVING THE SACRAMENTS

There are seven sacraments through which practising Catholics receive God's Grace. These are baptism, confirmation, the Eucharist, penance and reconciliation (popularly known as confession), "the anointing of the sick", holy orders and Holy Matrimony. According to the *Catechism of the Catholic Church*, the sacraments were "instituted by Christ and entrusted to the Church". They are stages in the spiritual life – from new birth as a Christian in baptism and confirmation, through to the anointing of the sick, often administered at the end of earthly life before the final journey into eternal life. The sacraments help individual Catholics make spiritual progress and grow in holiness.

Most people do not receive all seven sacraments: only some have a priestly vocation and receive holy orders, for example, and all who receive holy orders (except already married deacons) cannot receive Holy Matrimony. Individuals must be prepared to receive the sacraments. God's Grace may be blocked from working if someone is not disposed to receive it. For a sacrament to be effective, a person must have faith in it, although at the same time the sacraments in themselves strengthen and give expression to a person's faith.

Particular objects used by the clergy, including the special robes or vestments that a priest or bishop wears when celebrating the Eucharist or the Liturgy of the Hours, are termed "sacramentals". They are material things blessed or set apart to summon the respect believers should have for the sacraments of the Church – in the words of the *Baltimore Catechism* (a Catholic school text in the United States) "to excite good thoughts and increase devotion".

*Above The last rites performed for a dying person include celebration of the Eucharist, depicted in Hieronymus Bosch's 15th–16th-century painting Death and Last Rites.*

*Left The Eucharist is central among the sacraments. All seven sacraments are connected to Christ's paschal mystery – his redemptive sacrifice that is re-enacted in the Eucharist.*

# GOD'S HOUSE

THE FIRST CHRISTIANS WORSHIPPED IN PRIVATE HOUSES, BUT OVER
TIME CHURCHES HAVE DEVELOPED INTO SUBSTANTIAL PUBLIC
BUILDINGS THAT SERVE AS THE CENTRE OF ROMAN CATHOLIC LIFE.

The earliest public churches were built after Christianity was adopted as the state religion of the Roman Empire in the 4th century AD. They were based on the Roman basilica, a large roofed public building often used as a courthouse or market. Like the basilica, the early churches had a central hall, known as the nave, with a timber roof and an aisle on each side, which were separated from the nave by a line of columns.

A wooden altar was established toward one end of the nave. In the first churches, the altar was typically at the west end of the nave, in imitation of the arrangement in the Jewish Temple in Jerusalem. The bishop or

*Above The Jewish Temple in Jerusalem, shown in this c.1728 Jewish manuscript, was an inspiration to early Christians, who based part of their church layout on it.*

priest celebrating the Eucharist faced east – on the grounds that it was the direction of the heavenly Jerusalem and thus it was from this direction that Christ would return in glory – and so he always looked toward the congregation. For unknown reasons, in about the 6th century the arrangement was reversed, with the altar at the east end of the nave.

Beyond the altar was the apse, basically a semicircular or sometimes rectangular recess, usually vaulted, occupied by the bishop and priests during services. When celebrating the Eucharist, the bishop or priest, who continued to face east, looked toward the apse and away from the worshippers in the nave. The area around the altar, which was set aside for the clergy, became known as the presbytery or sanctuary.

*Left The west front of Lincoln Cathedral in England incorporates elements dating from 1072. The main part of the cathedral is 13th-century, in the Gothic style.*

At the west end, a long entrance porch called the narthex ran across the full width of the nave and led into the nave. Unbaptized believers and penitents generally remained in the narthex, where they were separated from clergy and other believers.

## THE BEMA AND THE CHOIR

There were many variations of these areas. In some churches, a wooden platform called the bema was built in the centre of the nave. The clergy sat in this area and read lessons and delivered sermons from the lectern on the bema. In some large churches, the eastern end of the nave began to be fenced off with a small railing to form an area for the choir, and sometimes the choir area was attached to the bema. This arrangement survives to this day in the Basilica di Santa Maria Maggiore (AD 430–40 ) in Rome. More typically, the choir area became a separate architectural feature connecting the nave and sanctuary.

## CRUCIFORM PLAN

In some churches, a transept was added on a north–south axis, perpendicular to the nave, to form a church shaped like a cross. The point at which the transept cuts across the nave was known as "the crossing": the nave usually extended to the west of the crossing and the choir and sanctuary lay to the east. The arms of the crossing were called north

*Above The altar stands at the centre of the Metropolitan Cathedral of Christ the King, Liverpool, England, surrounded on all sides by seats. The designer was aiming to help the congregation feel more linked to the liturgy.*

transept and south transept: at each end of these, additional altars were added in honour of particular saints. Often a dome was built above the crossing. A good example of this design is the magnificent 11th-century Basilica of San Michele Maggiore in Pavia, Italy. In some cathedrals – for instance at Lincoln (built 1092–1311) and Salisbury (1220–58), both in England – a second, smaller transept was built to the east of the main one.

## HALL CHURCH

In Italy in the 15th and 16th centuries, the hall church design was developed to reduce the long distance between entrance and altar. At this time, during the Counter-

Reformation (the Catholic Church's response to the rise of Protestantism), Church authorities wanted to promote the importance of preaching: a pulpit was introduced halfway down the nave and large side chapels were built nearby. A fine example of this design is the Church of the Gesù in Rome, the mother church of the Society of Jesus, or Jesuits, built in around 1568 by Giacomo da Vignola and Giacomo Della Porta.

## GREEK CHURCH DESIGN

From early times, many Eastern churches were built on the plan of a Greek cross – a cross with four arms of equal length. Rather than have the crossing toward one end of a long nave, these churches had four equally sized wings meeting at a central crossing. The crossing point was generally square and domed. One good example is the 6th-century Church of Hagia Sophia in Istanbul (which eventually became a mosque and is now a museum).

This design returned to relevance in Western churches of the late 20th century, many of which put the altar toward the centre of the church to symbolize the centrality of the Mass in Catholic life. Two examples include the Metropolitan Cathedral of Christ the King in Liverpool, England (1958–70), and the Cathedral of Saint Mary of the Assumption, which was built in San Francisco, California (1967–71).

## THE ROOD SCREEN AND REREDOS

In many medieval churches, a wooden screen separated the faithful in the nave from the clergy and other celebrants in the choir and sanctuary. The screen consisted of a large carved cross (or "rood") with an image of Jesus upon it, often flanked by carvings of the Blessed Virgin Mary and St John looking on. The structure was called the rood screen or choir screen. Many churches also had decorated screens behind the altar in the east. This often profoundly beautiful structure was called an altar piece or reredos.

*Right The intricately carved rood screen in the Gothic church of Saint-Etienne-du-Mont in Paris, France, has spiral staircases on either side.*

# GREAT CHURCHES

FROM ROME TO LOS ANGELES, FROM THE 4TH TO THE 21ST CENTURY, THE BASILICAS AND CATHEDRALS OF THE ROMAN CATHOLIC CHURCH ARE AMONG THE WORLD'S MOST INSPIRATIONAL BUILDINGS.

Traditionally, the apostle Peter went to Rome and became the Church's first bishop. He was martyred in Rome and was buried in a Christian cemetery on *Mons Vaticanus*, where the Vatican now stands. Emperor Constantine built a basilica on the site in AD 326–33. However, by the end of the 15th century this building was in poor condition.

## ST PETER'S BASILICA
The Basilica di San Pietro di Vaticano, better known as St Peter's Basilica, was built on the same site as the original basilica over more than a century, 1506–1626, and was consecrated in 1628. Among its many architects were Donato Bramante, Michelangelo and Gian Lorenzo Bernini. It stands within Vatican City – reputedly with St Peter's grave beneath its altar – and is considered the most holy church for Catholics

worldwide. Many popes, including John Paul II in 2005, have been buried in this basilica.

## MEDIEVAL CATHEDRALS
In the Middle Ages, the pope was often at odds with the Holy Roman emperor. During this time the great St Peter's Basilica in Rome was rivalled by the imperial church at Aachen (which is now part of western Germany), the most historic cathedral in northern Europe. At the heart of this church is the Palatine Chapel, which was founded by Charlemagne, King of the Franks, in 792 and consecrated to the Blessed Virgin Mary in 805 by Pope Leo III. German kings (and later emperors)

*Above The throne of Charlemagne on which Holy Roman emperors were crowned stands in the upper gallery of the Palatine Chapel in Aachen, Germany.*

were crowned in the Palatine Chapel for more than 600 years, between 936 and 1531.

Charlemagne himself was buried in a vault beneath the cathedral on his death in 814, and the cathedral became an attraction for pilgrims throughout the Middle Ages, when it was known as the Royal Church of St Mary at Aachen. The golden Shrine of St Mary was built in the choir in 1220–39 to contain four sacred relics: Christ's swaddling cloth, his loincloth, Mary's cloak and the beheading cloth of John the Baptist. Every seven years to the present day the relics are removed from the shrine and put on display for pilgrims.

There are other great European cathedrals of the Middle Ages and Renaissance, including the grand 13th-century Gothic cathedral of Chartres in France, celebrated for its magnificent stained-glass windows, and the Basilica di Santa Maria del Fiore, also known as Florence Cathedral, with its glorious 14th-century campanile (bell tower) partly designed by Giotto, the bronze doors of 1403–24 on the baptistery by

*Below Filippo Brunelleschi's breathtaking dome at Florence Cathedral contains 4 million bricks. With the lantern at its top, it is 114.5m (375ft) high.*

*Above The Basilica of Our Lady of Peace in Yamoussoukro, Ivory Coast, was built with the finest Italian marble as well as 7,000sq m (75,350sq ft) of stained glass.*

Lorenzo Ghiberti and the octagonal dome that was built in 1420–36 by Filippo Brunelleschi.

## MODERN RIVALS

The cathedral at Florence was built to rival St Peter's Basilica in size and grandeur, and this desire survived into the late 20th century. The Basilica of Our Lady of Peace in Yamoussoukro, Ivory Coast, Africa, was modelled on St Peter's, built in 1985–90 and consecrated by Pope John Paul II on 10 September 1990. It was designed to be the greatest Catholic church in the world: it covers a slightly larger area than St Peter's – 3 hectares (7.4 acres) compared to 2.3 hectares (5.7 acres). However, critics point out that the area includes a villa and rectory, which are not part of the church, and that the Ivory Coast basilica has a smaller capacity at 18,000 people, compared with 60,000 for St Peter's.

In Liverpool, England, the Metropolitan Cathedral of Christ the King was built in the 1960s to a design by Sir Frederick Gibberd. Its

*Above Light falling through the glass roof creates striking patterns in the Catedral Metropolitana Nossa Senhora Aparecida.*

circular plan was drawn up in response to the call by the Second Vatican Council for increased participation by the laity in the sacred liturgy. The cathedral was consecrated on the Feast of Pentecost, 14 May 1967. Another strikingly modern, circular cathedral is the Catedral Metropolitana Nossa Senhora Aparecida in Brasilia, Brazil. It was designed by Oscar Niemeyer, built from 1958 onward and was consecrated on 31 May 1970.

## OUR LADY OF THE ANGELS

The greatest Roman Catholic church dedicated in the early 21st century is surely the outwardly austere, inwardly beautiful Cathedral of Our Lady of the Angels in downtown Los Angeles, California. It was begun in 1997 to designs by Spanish architect José Rafael Moneo, and opened in September 2002. It incorporates a plaza of 1,860sq m (20,000sq ft) and a main sanctuary 100m (333ft) in length and up to 30m (100ft) high. It has superb bronze doors, created by artist Robert Graham, which pay homage across the centuries to Ghiberti's bronze doors in the Florence baptistery.

*Right The Cathedral of Our Lady of the Angels is 12 storeys high and is specially designed to resist earthquake damage.*

# THE ALTAR OF GOD

THE ALTAR, AT WHICH THE PRIEST CELEBRATES THE EUCHARIST, IS THE FOCAL POINT OF THE SANCTUARY. IT IS REVERED BY CHRISTIANS AS THE *MENSA DOMINI* ("TABLE OF THE LORD").

The sanctuary itself is the area set aside for the priest celebrant, deacons and other ministers. It is usually raised above the rest of the church, with its area demarcated by a low rail. Within the sanctuary, the altar is the principal furnishing. The altar represents the table at which Christ shared the Last Supper with his apostles and instituted the Eucharist.

The Church teaches that the altar also stands for Jesus himself and for the Cross on which his sacrifice was made: for these reasons, it is

*Above The altar stands in for the table used at the Last Supper by Christ and the apostles, which is shown in Domenico Ghirlandaio's 15th-century painting.*

honoured with incense. Numbers are often symbolic to Catholics, and the five crosses carved on it represent Jesus' Five Sacred Wounds.

The table or horizontal top of the altar is normally made of natural stone because it embodies Christ, described in the First Letter of Peter as "that living stone, rejected by men but in God's sight chosen and precious" (1 Peter 2:3–4). Although the support of the tabletop can be of any material, the altar should honour Christ by being simple and beautiful.

## SANCTIFIED BY RELICS

The altar stands on a raised platform called the predella. This is often made of wood. For symbolic reasons, the steps leading up to it are normally an uneven number – three, five or seven – and each about 15cm (6in) high. The steps may be of stone, wood or

*Left Three steps mount to the main altar in St Patrick's Cathedral, New York City. The sanctuary was renovated in the 1930s to 1940s, when the elegant baldacchino (canopy) was added.*

brick. If there are three steps, they are used to distinguish between ranks of ministers at the Eucharist: the celebrant will stand on the predella, the deacon on the second step and a subdeacon or another lower-ranking minister on the third step.

Beneath the altar is a box called the sepulchrum, used for containing a holy relic and other specific objects. The box has a gold, silver or lead reliquary to hold part of the bodily remains of a saint, together with three grains of incense and a parchment certifying that the altar has been consecrated. If possible, the relic is of the saint in whose name the church was built. The relics were traditionally placed within the altar, but they are now set beneath it. Catholics do not worship the relics or saints. The saints are honoured as men and women of great holiness, exemplars of the Christian life. The relics remind believers that the Eucharist celebrated on the altar is a source of God's Grace, the grace that enabled the saints to live such holy lives.

## MARKING A CELEBRATION

For a celebration three white cloths are laid on the altar. Two candles are lighted to celebrate a Low Mass, one

*Below A burning candle marks the presence of the blessed sacrament within the tabernacle (centre). Its presence further sanctifies the altar as the table of the Lord.*

spoken by a priest without incense or the presence of a deacon or sub-deacon; but six candles are required for a High Mass, a solemn celebration with music.

## THE TABERNACLE

The gifts of the bread and the wine are consecrated during the Mass and distributed to the people. Some consecrated bread and wine – the blessed sacrament – is reserved in the tabernacle, a small carved metal container. The tabernacle is usually kept within the sanctuary, on the altar or at the side, but in some churches it is kept in a separate side chapel. It is sometimes kept beneath a small canopy or conopaeum.

A candle must always be kept burning above the tabernacle. This is called the altar lamp, or sanctuary light. The light reminds the faithful of the presence of Christ in the blessed sacrament and it embodies Christ, called in the Gospel of John "the true light that enlightens every man" (John 1:9). The light is an expression of the burning love of the faithful for their Lord. Although more than one light may be on the tabernacle, there are always uneven numbers lit: three, five, seven and so on.

## GOSPEL AND SERMONS

In many churches, a raised pulpit stands at the front of the sanctuary, on the left-hand side of the church as

you face the altar. The gospel and sermons or homilies are traditionally delivered from this pulpit. On the right-hand side of the sanctuary as you face the altar is usually a lectern, from which the Epistle is generally read. Although lay people can use the lectern, only members of the clergy can use the pulpit. Some churches do not have pulpit and lectern. Instead, they have a single podium, called an ambo, in the space otherwise occupied by the pulpit.

*Above The sanctuary of the 13th-century St Asaph Cathedral in Denbighshire, North Wales, contains the bishop's seat.*

# VESTMENTS

WHEN CELEBRATING THE LITURGY OF THE CATHOLIC CHURCH, MEMBERS OF THE CLERGY WEAR SPECIAL ROBES OR VESTMENTS THAT SYMBOLIZE ASPECTS OF A PRIEST'S SPIRITUAL ROLE.

The celebrant's vestments distinguish him from the people and remind him of his vocation and duties, and the holiness of the acts he undertakes. The wearing of priestly vestments has historical roots going right back to the early days of Christianity – and even beyond to the Old Testament age, when the Jewish priests of Aaron wore ritual garb.

To celebrate the liturgy and in processions, clerics traditionally wear a cassock, a long, close-fitting cloak with buttons down the front, so-called from the Italian *casacca* for "greatcoat". Priests generally wear a black cassock, while bishops wear a purple one and cardinals a red one (or a black one with red piping). The pope's cassock is always white.

## VESTMENTS FOR EUCHARIST

To celebrate the Eucharist, a priest also wears an alb, a cincture, a stole and a chasuble. An alb is a full-length white linen gown worn over the priest's cassock. It is a descendant of the white toga worn by the ancient Romans and takes its name from the Latin word *albus*, meaning "white". The alb's colour symbolizes purity. Around the waist the priest secures the alb with a braided linen or woollen cord called the cincture, from the Latin *cinctura*, meaning "girdle". It is usually white, like the alb. The cincture is worn to symbolize the priest's chastity.

Around his neck and across his shoulders, the priest wears a long decorated strip of material called a stole. It should be approximately 200cm (80in) long and 5–10cm (2–4in) in width. The stole generally has a cross embroidered at each end and in the middle (the part worn behind the neck); the middle cross is required because the priest must

*Below Kneeling deacons wear the alb (full-length white gown), cincture (cord belt) and stole (strip across shoulder and chest).*

*Above Many priests still wear a black cassock for day-to-day duties, but some wear a suit with shirt and clerical collar.*

kiss this when putting on the stole. Bishops wear the stole in the same manner as priests; deacons wear it over the left shoulder and diagonally across the chest.

The priest wears a decorated outer garment called the chasuble over his vestments. The chasuble is usually made of silk or velvet and often has a large cross on the back. Its name derives from the Latin *casula*, which means "little house", because the over garment provides protection or shelter for the priest. The chasuble symbolizes the yoke of Christ and the virtue of charity.

## THE AMICE AND MANIPLE

Beneath the alb the priest can choose to wear an amice over his shoulders. The amice is a rectangular white cloth, marked with a cross and attached to two long ribbon-like strings, which are used to secure it. It takes its name from the Latin *amictus*, meaning "cloak" or "mantle". Wearing an amice was once compulsory for priests celebrating the Eucharist, but when liturgical reforms were introduced in 1972 wearing an amice became voluntary. Today many priests choose to wear one in honour of tradition.

The priest may also choose to wear a maniple. This is a long and narrow embroidered strip of material traditionally worn over the left arm. For most priests the maniple is an optional vestment, but those who celebrate the Extraordinary Form of the Roman Rite (the Tridentine Mass) are required to wear it when celebrating the Eucharist.

## OTHER VESTMENTS

In liturgical settings other than the Mass, a priest may wear the cope, humeral veil and surplice. The cope is a very long and often heavy embroidered mantle or cloak worn over the shoulder, reaching to the ankles, and fastened at the chest with an often highly decorated clasp called a morse. The cope, which takes its name from the Latin *cappa* ("cape"), is often worn in processions and at benedictions (a service in which the blessed sacrament is exposed on the altar in a monstrance, or vessel, for the adoration of the faithful), as well as for many other solemn liturgical offices other than the Mass.

The humeral veil is also traditionally worn at benediction: it is a long piece of usually richly ornamented material worn over the shoulders and covering the hands of the priest. Priests also wear it when carrying sacred vessels containing the reserved sacrament in a procession.

## LITURGICAL COLOURS

Priests celebrate Mass in vestments of different colours according to the season of the church year or to mark a particular saint's day or festival. The four main colours are white, red, green and purple; in addition, on more solemn days festive silver and gold vestments can also be worn – silver in place of white, and gold in place of white, red or green.

White symbolizes purity and the glory of the Resurrection and is the colour for the Easter season; it is also worn on major feast days, such as Christmas Day and Easter Day, feasts of the Blessed Virgin Mary and of saints who were confessors or virgins. Purple symbolizes repentance and is worn for Lent and Advent. Red, as the colour of blood, is worn on the feast days of saints who were martyred; as the colour of fire, it is worn on Pentecost, the festival commemorating the descent of the Holy Spirit as tongues of fire (Acts 2:3). Green is worn on ordinary days – that is, times of the year that are not part of a particular church season and not feast days. Green stands for the growth of the Church.

*Above* Clergy in procession at Lourdes, France, prior to a Mass for the sick wear the cope or long clerical cloak.

The surplice is basically a half-length tunic usually made of cotton or linen and sometimes featuring an embroidered hem and sleeves. It is worn over the cassock when administering sacraments other than the Eucharist and when saying the Liturgy of the Hours, as well as during processions.

*Right* Because this priest is celebrating the Eucharist, he is wearing a chasuble (the heavy, ornately decorated outer garment), which is worn over his alb, cincture and stole.

# "GATHERED TOGETHER IN MY NAME"

IN THE FIRST PART OF THE SACRAMENT OF THE EUCHARIST, READINGS AND A HOMILY FORM THE LITURGY OF THE WORD, WHICH PREPARES THE FAITHFUL TO RECEIVE HOLY COMMUNION.

The Catholic celebration of the Eucharist is known as the Mass, from the word *missa*. This is used as a form of dismissal at the close of the traditional Latin form of the service: *Ite, missa est* ("Go, it is finished"). The Mass is a sacramental re-enactment of the death and Resurrection of Jesus, in which bread and wine become the body and blood of Christ and are offered to God again, just as they were on the Cross. In this sacrament, the community of believers makes symbolic expression of its unity and is nourished by receiving Jesus' body and blood.

Mass was originally said in Latin, but the Second Vatican Council (1962–5) allowed conferences of bishops to make their own judgement on the extent to which English

*Below The bread that Jesus broke during the Last Supper with his apostles can be seen in Girolamo di Romano's 16th-century painting* The Last Supper.

or other local vernacular languages could be used. The great majority of Masses are today celebrated in approved vernacular translations, but Latin is still used occasionally and in some places is used regularly.

## ENTRANCE AND GREETING

On entering, the priest kisses the altar and, when incense is used, he censes it. All present make a large sign of the Cross, using the fingertips of the open right hand to touch forehead, chest, left shoulder, then right shoulder, while the priest says "In the name of the Father, and of the Son, and of the Holy Spirit: Amen."

The priest extends both hands and, facing the people, welcomes them with one of a series of greetings based on the beginnings of the Epistles of St Paul. They respond. In the simplest form of the greeting, the priest says "The Lord be with you", and the people respond "And also with you".

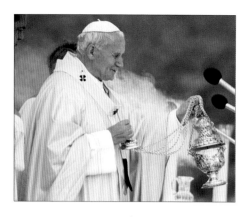

*Above Pope John Paul II censes the altar during a Mass in Switzerland in 1984. He uses a thurible (metal censer).*

## ACT OF PENITENCE

The priests call on those present to take part in the act of penitence. The most common form is the Confiteor, or Mea Culpa, said by all. It begins:

> *I confess to Almighty God, and to you, my brothers and sisters, that I have sinned through my own fault in my thoughts and in my words...*

When the congregation says "through my own fault", it is customary for them to strike themselves on the chest. The act of penitence concludes with the priest praying, "May almighty God have mercy on us, forgive us our sins, and bring us to everlasting life."

All present then usually say or sing the Kyrie Eleison, either in English ("Lord have mercy, Christ have mercy, Lord have mercy") or the original Greek (*Kyrie Eleison, Christe Eleison, Kyrie Eleison*). The threefold repetition is in veneration of the Trinity of Father, Son and Holy Spirit. Afterward, all join in singing or saying the ancient hymn of *Gloria in Excelsis Deo*, which begins "Glory to God in the highest, and peace to his people on earth..."

## LITURGY OF THE WORD

The priest invites all to pray and after a period of silent prayer, he reads the set collect (a collection of short

prayers) for the day. Biblical readings follow with three on Sundays and solemn occasions, two on other days. The first is from the Old Testament and is usually followed by a psalm. The second is from the New Testament, generally one of the Epistles to early Christians. On both occasions, the reader declares on finishing "This is the Word of the Lord" and the congregation responds "Thanks be to God".

## THE HOLY GOSPEL

The third reading is from the Holy Gospel. This is read by a deacon, or by the priest if no deacon is present. Before the Gospel an hallelujah, or expression of praise to God, is sung or said. The deacon or priest declares "The Lord be with you", to which the people respond, "And also with you"; he announces "A reading from the Holy Gospel according to…" and makes a sign of the cross over the Bible and on his own forehead, lips and chest; the people do likewise and make the response "Glory to you, Lord". When incense is used, the priest or deacon censes the book. At the end of the reading he declares "This is the Gospel of the Lord", and the congregation responds "Praise to you, Lord Jesus Christ". The priest or deacon then kisses the book.

*Left As the high point of the liturgy of the Word, a priest delivers a reading from the Holy Gospel.*

## ENDING WITH A PRAYER

A bishop, priest or deacon usually delivers a homily or sermon, then all present recite the Nicene Creed, which begins: "We believe in one God, the Father, the Almighty…" The liturgy of the Word concludes with the Prayers of the Faithful: a deacon, cantor or member of the congregation leads all in prayer requests before the priest declaims a concluding prayer.

### HOLY WATER

On Sundays, and especially during the Easter season, the rite of asperges – the blessing and sprinkling of holy water – is sometimes used in place of the act of penitence and the Kyrie. The priest explains that the water is to remind all present of their baptism.

One of several prayers available includes the phrase "Lord in your mercy give us living water, always springing up as a fountain of salvation: free us, body and soul, from every danger…". The priest then takes the aspergil (silver water sprinkler) and sprinkles first himself, then the other clergy and then the people present with the holy water. While he does this, an antiphon or hymn is sung.

*Above A priest pours out water prior to blessing and sprinkling it in the rite of asperges.*

*Left Priests sing "We praise Thee, We bless Thee, We worship Thee, We glorify Thee" as they lead the gloria during Mass.*

# THE MOST HOLY SACRAMENT OF THE ALTAR

THE SECOND PART OF THE MASS IS THE LITURGY OF THE EUCHARIST, IN WHICH THE BREAD AND WINE ARE CONSECRATED AND DISTRIBUTED TO THE COMMUNICANTS AS THE BODY AND BLOOD OF JESUS CHRIST.

In the first section of the liturgy, the bread and wine that will be used in the Eucharist are brought to the altar, usually by members of the congregation in a formal procession. They usually sing an offertory hymn.

The priest prays over the gifts of bread and wine. He places the bread on a small silver or gold plate called the paten and mixes water and wine in a precious cup, referred to as the chalice. When incense is being used, the priest censes the offerings and the altar, and a deacon or other minister censes the priest and the people. The priest then washes his hands, symbolizing his desire for inner purification.

*Above* At the sacred climax of the Eucharist, a bishop holds the consecrated Host aloft to show it to the congregation.

## EUCHARISTIC PRAYER

The Eucharistic Prayer leads the congregation through the sacred climax of the Eucharist, in which the bread and the wine are consecrated and become Christ's body and blood. There are variations of the prayer. The key elements, found in all versions, are when making a sign of the Cross over the bread and the wine, the priest blesses the offerings on the altar and recalls how Christ instituted the Eucharist at the Last Supper.

The priest copies Christ's actions as he recounts how Christ took the bread in his sacred hands, looked to heaven, gave thanks and praise to God the Father, and then broke the bread, giving it to his disciples, and said, "Take this, all of you, and eat it", then referring to it as his body, "which will be given up for you". At this point, the bread is made holy and becomes the consecrated Host, the very body of Christ. An acolyte often rings a bell to signal the holy moment, and if incense is being used

*Left In Ingres' 1866 painting,* Virgin of the Eucharist, *the Blessed Virgin Mary contemplates the divine mystery of her son's presence in the Host.*

he censes the priest and the paten. The priest lifts the Host and then places it back on the paten on the altar and kneels in adoration.

The priest raises the chalice and recounts Christ's actions in taking a cup of wine, giving thanks and praise to the Father in heaven, then giving it to the disciples, stating, "Take this all of you and drink from it". The priest refers to the contents in the cup as "the blood of the new and everlasting covenant" and continues by stating that blood was shed for humankind so that its sins will be forgiven. At this point, an acolyte once again rings a bell to signal the moment of consecration, and if incense is being used, he will cense the priest and chalice.

## COMMUNION RITE

Before the congregation receives the Eucharist, all join in repeating the Lord's Prayer, then they share a sign of peace according to local custom. The priest breaks the Host and puts a piece in the chalice in what is called the rite of fraction, and prays: "May this mingling of the body and blood of our Lord Jesus Christ bring eternal life to all who receive it."

*Below In today's Mass, communicants receive the consecrated Host when the priest places it on the tongue.*

*Above Incense signifies the sanctity of the altar and of the gifts of bread and wine that become the Lord's body and blood.*

The priest says a prayer of personal devotion, then presents the Host (consecrated bread) to the congregation with the words, "This is the Lamb of God who takes away the sins of the world. Happy are those who are called to his supper."All present respond with the words, "Lord I am not worthy to receive you" and finish off with "say the word and I shall be healed".

The priest receives Communion himself and distributes it to other ministers and deacons, and then to the congregation, who usually come forward in procession. Each communicant bows, then receives the Host on the tongue (in the past it was sometimes received in the hand); the priest declares "the body of Christ" and the communicant responds "Amen". The communicant is offered the chalice and the priest declares "the blood of Christ".

It is possible for communicants to receive only the Host, and for the priest to dip the Host into the wine and present it in that form, laying it on the communicant's tongue; this is called intinction. Usually, the congregation sings a Communion song throughout this period.

Afterward, the chalice, paten and other vessels are washed and dried and placed on the altar and the priest declaims a prayer after Communion. At this point notices are read out, then the priest gives one of a choice of blessings on the people and pronounces one of a choice of dismissals. All include the phrase "Go in peace"; the variant based on the original Latin dismissal (*Ite, missa est*), which gives the Mass its name, is "The Mass is ended. Go in peace". The congregation responds, "Thanks be to God."Then the priest kisses the altar, makes a customary reverence with other ministers and leaves. A hymn is often sung at the close of the service.

# BAPTISM

IN THE SACRAMENT OF BAPTISM, AN INDIVIDUAL IS REBORN AS A
CHRISTIAN AND GAINS A SANCTIFYING GRACE THAT ENABLES HIM OR
HER TO SHARE IN THE LIFE OF GOD – FATHER, SON AND HOLY SPIRIT.

Most Catholics are baptized as
infants, but those who convert to
Catholicism can be baptized as an
adult if they have not previously been
baptized in another Christian
denomination. With confirmation
and Holy Communion, baptism is
listed as one of three sacraments of
initiation that prepares an individual
for life as a Christian.

According to the *Catechism of
the Catholic Church*, baptism is the
backbone of the complete Christian
life, "the gateway to life in the spirit";
through baptism people are united
with Christ and are "incorporated

*Below Our Lord explains the necessity
of being "born of water and the Spirit" to
Nicodemus, depicted in this 17th-century
painting by Crijn Hendricksz Volmarijn.*

into the Church and made sharers in
Her mission". In baptism, people join
the priesthood of believers.

## A NEW BIRTH
One of the key biblical texts that
supports baptism is from Jesus'
words to Nicodemus, "Truly, truly,
I say to you, unless one is born of
water and the Spirit, he cannot enter
the kingdom of God" (John 3:5).
Baptism is a symbolic rebirth: and
only through baptism can believers
come to the other sacraments of
Christian life.

According to Catholic doctrine,
baptism frees an individual from
original sin (the mark of human sin-
fulness with which all are tainted, and
which derives from the disobedience
to God's commandments of the first

*Above When Jesus was baptized by
John the Baptist, the Holy Spirit
descended upon him. Perugino captured
the scene in this c. 1500 painting,*
Baptism of Christ in the Jordan.

people, Adam and Eve, in the Garden
of Eden). For this reason, practising
Catholics believe they must baptize
their children as infants; should the
children die unbaptized, they would
remain tainted by original sin and
their salvation would be prevented.
Baptism also liberates people from
their own sins and from any punishment deriving from these.

## RITE OF BAPTISM
In normal circumstances, the rite of
baptism involves friends or relatives
of the child's parents as "godparents";
they hold a responsibility to help the
parents in raising the baptized child
as a Christian. The bishop, priest or
deacon greets both the parents and
godparents and reminds them of
the responsibilities attendant on
bringing an infant to baptism, which
include training the infant "in the
practice of the faith" and keeping
God's commandments "as Christ
taught us, by loving God and our

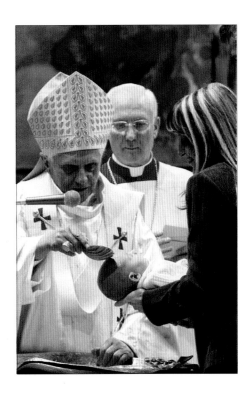

*Above An infant is baptized by Pope Benedict XVI. The catechism teaches that by being baptized "we are freed from sin and reborn as sons of God".*

neighbour". He then leads the parents (and godparents if desired) in tracing the Cross of Christ on the infant's forehead.

Readings from the Holy Gospel and a homily or sermon follow. The celebrant leads the prayer of the faithful that calls on God to "bathe this child in light" and give the child "new life of baptism" and asks that the child is welcomed into the holy

Church. The prayers also call on God to "renew the grace of our baptism in each one of us".

The celebrant invokes the Blessed Virgin and the saints, and proceeds to a prayer of exorcism and anointing before baptism in which he calls on God to free the child from original sin and "make him (or her) a temple of your glory". He then anoints the infant with oil in Christ's name.

## SACRED WATERS

At the font, the celebrant recites an introductory prayer. The priest blesses the water in the font, then once again reminds the parents and godparents of their responsibility to raise the infant in the Catholic faith. He asks them to make three professions of their faith: in God the Father; in Jesus Christ; and in the Holy Spirit. As he says this he refers to the Catholic Church and the communion of saints, as well as Jesus' Resurrection and everlasting life. All present then announce their belief in these things: "This is our faith. This is the faith of the Church." They then declare that they are proud of their profession.

Then the celebrant baptizes the infant, saying the child's name and declaring, "I baptize you in the name of the Father and of the Son and of the Holy Spirit." At each naming of God, he either pours water over

*Above A Catholic convert leans over a font as she is baptized in the Cathedral of Notre-Dame de Paris – the celebrant is using a traditional scallop shell.*

the infant's forehead or immerses the child in the water of the font. The celebrant anoints the infant with chrism, or holy oil, and clothes him or her in a white garment as an "outward sign of Christian dignity". The baptism usually concludes with the celebrant reaffirming that the infant has been reborn in baptism, leading the congregation in the Lord's Prayer, then giving a blessing.

## SYMBOLIC WATER

When the main baptism takes place at the font, the celebrant's introductory prayer identifies water as a symbol of God's grace and a "wellspring of holiness". The waters of baptism are likened to those that existed before the Creation and on which God breathed, to those of Noah's flood, to the waters of the Red Sea that parted as the Israelites were led out of Egypt, to those of the Jordan in which Christ himself was baptized and to the waters mixed with blood that flowed from his side on the Cross.

*Right A font holds holy water used for baptism – this 12th-century Belgian font depicts Jesus' own baptism.*

# CONFIRMATION

PEOPLE WHO RECEIVE THE SACRAMENT OF CONFIRMATION ARE ANOINTED WITH HOLY OIL. THE RITE CONFIRMS AND STRENGTHENS THE GRACE THEY DERIVED FROM BAPTISM.

Confirmation is the second of the three sacraments of initiation, and is traditionally delivered after baptism and before the Eucharist. In the early Church and the Eastern Church today, these three sacraments are delivered in a single occasion in early childhood, but in the Western Church (in the Latin Rite) confirmation is delayed until late childhood, at a time when the recipient can understand the significance of the sacrament. When adults are baptized, they usually receive the three sacraments at the same time and in the traditional order.

In most cases in the Western Church, only a bishop can administer the sacrament of confirmation, but priests have been authorized to confirm adult converts and children who are at risk of death; the priest uses chrism or holy oil blessed by the

*Below The laying on of hands is a key part of confirmation. As descendants of the apostles, bishops perform the rite.*

bishop. The chrism is blessed in a special service, the Chrism Mass, on Holy Thursday during Easter Week.

## THE GIFT OF THE SPIRIT

The Church places an emphasis on the connection between confirmation and the Feast of Pentecost, when the Holy Spirit descended on Christ's apostles. Bishops, as successors to the apostles, administer confirmation. There is also a biblical precedent for the practice of bishops imparting the Holy Spirit to others through the laying on of hands. Acts 8:15–17 describes when the apostles Peter and John went to the Christians in Samaria and "prayed for them that they might receive the Holy Spirit, for it had not yet fallen upon any of them; they had only been baptized in the name of the Lord Jesus. Then they laid hands on them and they received the Holy Spirit."

In the Latin Rite used by the Western Catholic Church, the confirmation service begins with those

*Above A bishop anoints candidates for confirmation with chrism, signifying the mark of the Holy Spirit, in this 15th-century painting by Rogier van der Weyden.*

ready for confirmation, known as confirmands, renewing their baptismal vows and professing their faith. The bishop extends his hands over them and prays: "All-powerful God, Father of our Lord Jesus Christ, by water and the Holy Spirit you freed your sons and daughters from sin and gave them new life…". Then he anoints each confirmand with chrism. The bishop says, "Be sealed with the gift of the Holy Spirit." The anointing is accompanied by a laying on of hands by the bishop. The phrase "be sealed" signifies that the newly confirmed belongs to Christ in God. The seal marks the Christian as being enrolled in Christ's service and also provides a promise of divine protection. At the close of the service the bishop makes the sign of peace over the newly confirmed Christians.

In the Eastern Catholic Church, a priest generally administers the sacraments of baptism, confirmation

(usually referred to as Chrismation) and Communion in a single ceremony. The priest will use chrism blessed by the bishop, anointing the recipient on the forehead, eyes, nose, ears, lips, breast, back, hands and feet, each time, declaring "The seal of the gift that is the Holy Spirit".

## ITS BENEFITS

The sacrament is called confirmation in the Western Church because it confirms, completes, strengthens and deepens the grace imparted by baptism. In confirmation, according to the catechism, baptized members of the faithful are "more perfectly bound to the Church", "enriched with a special strength of the Holy Spirit" and thereby "more strictly obliged to spread and defend the faith by word and deed".

The sacrament connects believers "more firmly to Christ" and unites the faithful in "divine filiation" (the condition of being a child of God). While baptism brings Christians into the priesthood of believers, confirmation perfects this priesthood and, according to St Thomas Aquinas, "The confirmed person receives the power to profess faith in Christ publicly and as it were officially (*quasi ex officio*)."

## FIRST COMMUNION

In the Western Church, the occasion on which a young person receives Holy Communion (when he or she participates in the Eucharist) for the first time, is often celebrated with a family party. Especially in the United States and Ireland, these celebrations can be lavish: boys dress in a suit and girls wear a special white dress with a veil and gloves. In some countries, a girl wears a dress handed down from her mother or sister; in others, she will take First Communion in school uniform plus veil and gloves. In many Latin American countries, boys dress in a uniform with military-style aigullettes (braided cords) for the ceremony.

## CONFIRMATION AFTER FIRST COMMUNION

The traditional order in which the three sacraments of initiation were received was: baptism, confirmation, Communion. However, in the early 20th century, Pope Pius X encouraged Catholics to allow children to receive the Eucharist as soon as they reached the age of reason (generally understood to be about the age of seven years). As a result, many young people received Communion before they were confirmed. However, in the late 20th and early 21st centuries, there has been a return to the traditional order.

*Above* Girls wear white dresses, sometimes with veils and gloves, for first Communion. The colour symbolizes their purity.

It is also traditional for the young person to receive a present to mark the occasion – perhaps a prayer book, icon or rosary.

*Below* The Eastern Catholic Church emphasizes the Christian initiation by delivering baptism, Chrismation (confirmation) and the Eucharist together.

# HOLY MATRIMONY

THE SACRAMENT OF HOLY MATRIMONY GIVES A COUPLE THE DIVINE GRACE THEY NEED TO ACHIEVE HOLINESS IN THEIR MARRIED LIFE. THE "AUTHOR" OF THE MARRIAGE IS GOD.

In marriage, husband and wife receive the Holy Spirit, which helps the married couple to keep their vows. As the *Catechism of the Catholic Church* puts it, "The Holy Spirit is the seal of their covenant, the ever available source of their love and the strength to renew their fidelity."

## WITNESS TO THE UNION

In the Latin Rite of the Western Church, the wedding ceremony takes place before a priest and at least two witnesses: strictly speaking, the ministers of Christ's Grace in this sacrament are the husband and wife, and the priest is a witness. However,

*Above In the Eastern Catholic Church, the sacrament is called the "Crowning". The crowns worn by bride and bridegroom are a sign of the marriage covenant.*

in the Eastern Catholic Church, the minister of the sacrament will be the presiding bishop or priest, who crowns husband and wife. There are two variants of the Latin Rite Catholic marriage ceremony: one with Mass, lasting about one hour, and one without Mass, which lasts around 20 minutes.

## RITE OF MARRIAGE

When both husband and wife are Catholics, they are encouraged by the Church to have a wedding Mass. The priest usually meets the couple at the door of the church and leads them to the altar. The next stage is to celebrate the liturgy of the Word, in the course of which the priest delivers a homily on the mystery of marriage, the responsibilities of husband and wife and the dignity of love between a married couple.

Then the priest begins the rite of marriage. He addresses the couple: "You have come together in this church so that the Lord may seal and strengthen your love in the presence of the Church's minister and this community." He will question the

*Left Catholic marriages are usually celebrated during Holy Mass. In their marriage, bride and bridegroom are inspired by Jesus' self-sacrifice. They become one body in Christ.*

couple's condition and intentions, asking them to confirm that they are joining "freely and without reservations", that they will "love and honour each other as man and wife for the rest of [their] lives" and that they will accept children from God and bring them up in the law of Christ and his Church.

Then the couple exchange vows, each promising "to be true…in good times and in bad, in sickness and in health" and declaring, "I will love and honour you all the days of my life". The words of the vows may vary. The priest blesses the couple, asking Jesus to strengthen their consent and fill them with blessings. The priest then blesses the rings and the couple exchange rings, which are worn as a sign of mutual love and fidelity.

## NUPTIAL BLESSING

The service proceeds by way of general intercessions into the liturgy of the Eucharist. After the Lord's

*Above Joseph and Mary exchange rings in this 14th-century detail of* Wedding of the Virgin Mary *by Bartolo di Fredi. From early on, the Catholic Church has taught that couples should love with a "supernatural…and fruitful love".*

*Below God blesses married love; its purpose is for procreation. A married couple receive a child from God in this 15th-century French miniature.*

Prayer the priest proclaims the nuptial blessing, calling on Jesus to bless bride and groom individually and as a couple joined in a holy bond and married in Christ to one another. The priest reminds all that marriage is a holy mystery that symbolizes the marriage of Christ to his Church, the one blessing of those given to Adam and Eve that was not "forfeited by original sin or washed away in the flood", and asks that the husband trust his wife and recognize that "she is his equal and heir with him to the life of grace". The priest prays, if the woman is of childbearing age, that the couple be blessed with children and have a long life, and after happy old age achieve fullness of life with the saints in heaven.

Then the couple receive Holy Communion. At the end of the service the priest blesses them once more before husband and wife kiss. All sing a hymn as the couple process out of the church. When a couple chooses a marriage service without Holy Communion it largely follows the outline above, but omits the celebration of the Eucharist.

### SPECIAL DISPENSATION

Those who come forward for marriage should normally be baptized Catholics. However, a dispensation, usually granted by the priest himself, is possible for a "mixed marriage" between a Catholic and a baptized non-Catholic (a Christian of another denomination) as long as the couple have chosen freely to marry, have the intention of remaining together for life and being faithful to one another, and are planning to have children if the bride has not passed the childbearing age. If one partner is Catholic and the other is not baptized (perhaps a non-Christian or a person of no religion), a church dispensation for disparity of cult is required from the local bishop.

# "WHAT GOD HAS JOINED..."

FOR CATHOLICS, HOLY MATRIMONY CREATES A PERMANENT AND INDISSOLUBLE BOND BETWEEN HUSBAND AND WIFE. GOD CREATED MARRIAGE AS THE FULFILMENT OF LIFE FOR MOST MEN AND WOMEN.

As part of the blessing of the married couple during the sacrament of Holy Matrimony, the priest may state, "What God has joined together, let no man put asunder", which is a direct quotation from Christ's own teaching on marriage (Mark 10:9). The *Catechism of the Catholic Church* is also unequivocal, stating that once a marriage between a baptized couple has been consummated, it "can never be dissolved".

Like the other sacraments, Holy Matrimony has both outward and inward signs: the outward sign is the marriage contract, which is the

*Below By participating in the wedding at Cana in Galilee, shown in this 14th-century painting,* The Marriage Feast at Cana, *by Duccio di Buoninsegna, Jesus confirmed the holiness of the marriage bond.*

agreement made verbally between both husband and wife when they exchange vows before the priest and witnesses; the inward sign is the grace it delivers. The Church's teaching accepts that marriage can bring many challenges; however, it also stresses that God's Grace is sufficient to help husbands and wives over-come their difficulties.

## DIVINE INSTITUTION

The Church teaches that God created man and woman for one another and that married love is in the image of God's love. Christ attended the wedding at Cana in Galilee, where he performed the first of the many signs that confirmed his status as the Son of God by turning water into wine (John 2:1–11). The Church interprets this event as confirmation

*Above A blessing is given to both man and woman in this 15th-century detail from* Engagement of the Virgin *by Michael Pacher. Both must freely give their consent to be married.*

of the goodness of marriage and a proclamation that marriage is a sign of Christ's presence.

For Catholics, marriage is both a natural and a divine institution. It is a natural institution because it has existed in the form of a lifelong union between a man and a woman in all societies and cultures through history. Yet it is also a divine insti-tution created by God, sanctified by Christ at Cana, and sealed through the sacrament of Holy Matrimony by the action of the Holy Spirit.

## IN PREPARATION

The Church instructs that both parties to a marriage must have a clear understanding of what they are doing when they take their marriage vows. Husband and wife are required to attend preparatory meetings with the priest who will witness their marriage. These meetings are known as pre-Cana meetings – a reference to the wedding at Cana.

A course of pre-Cana meetings can be held over a single weekend or be spread over six months or so.

## ANNULMENT OF A MARRIAGE

The key condition for a marriage is that husband and wife give their consent to be married freely and are free to give their consent. In cases where the parties to a marriage can show that either of these conditions were not met, a Church tribunal can grant an annulment of the marriage. Annulment is not the same as divorce: the judgement does not dissolve the marriage, for marriage is an indissoluble bond; it determines that the marriage did not ever take place.

The two parties must understand what they are doing and must have given the matter some consideration; they must have a genuine intention to keep the vows they swear – to form a permanent and faithful union, inclusive of sexual acts intended for the purpose of procreation. Various impediments to the marriage are grounds for annulment. Examples include husband and wife being close blood relatives, one partner being already married at the time of the wedding or one partner being in a psychological state that precludes an ability to give free consent.

*Right Henry VIII's wife Catherine of Aragon is shown in* The Divorce of Henry VIII, *by Eugene Deveria. Theirs was one of several marriages Henry had annulled.*

The priest and the married couple discuss the sanctity of marriage, their faith and life in the Church, plans for children and so on; they may be asked about financial matters. Nearer to the time, husband and wife, if both are baptized Catholics, are expected to receive the sacrament of penance and reconciliation in preparation for their wedding. With these preparations, both husband and wife should enter marriage prepared to maintain their vows – married life should present no surprises.

### WHEN A MARRIAGE FAILS

The Church recognizes that in some cases a marriage can deteriorate so badly that husband and wife can no longer live together. In this situation, they should live separately and the members of the Church should help them live as best they can in a Christian fashion. The estranged husband and wife are not free to divorce or remarry, and they should remember that the preferred solution in the eyes of the Catholic Church would be for the couple to reconcile their differences.

If a Catholic divorces and makes a second (civil) marriage, the Church views the person as committing adultery against the first marriage partner. He or she is in contravention of God's law and cannot receive the Eucharist. Nevertheless, that person should be welcomed to church if he or she wants to come: priests and the whole Church community should be attentive toward that person.

*Right God intends man and woman to join permanently in marriage; once joined, they should not seek separation. A 19th-century engraving,* The Ages of Life, *shows how a married couple honour their vows throughout life.*

# THE SANCTITY OF LIFE

CHURCH TEACHINGS ON MARRIAGE, SEX AND CONTRACEPTION, ABORTION AND HOMOSEXUALITY ARE UNDERPINNED BY BELIEF IN THE SANCTITY OF ALL LIVES CREATED BY GOD.

The Catholic faithful believe that sex has a divinely ordained place within a couple's marriage: its purpose and function is for the procreation of children. Married love is blessed by God and meant to be fruitful. This teaching is based on verses in Genesis, Chapter 1:

> *So God created man in his own*
> *image, in the image of God he*
> *created him; male and female*
> *he created them. And God blessed*
> *them, and God said to them,*
> *"Be fruitful and multiply, and*
> *fill the earth and subdue it."*
> *(Genesis 1:26–29).*

### AT THE SERVICE OF LIFE

Parents are called not only to procreate but also to educate: having brought children into the world, they must give them instruction in moral and spiritual matters. Parents should serve their children in love. The *Catechism of the Catholic Church* states

*Below The pope holds a fatherly position to Catholics. Married couples entrust their children to the care of God and his Church.*

that one of the main functions of marriage and family is "to be at the service of life".

There are some married couples who have not had children, but this does not devalue their marriage in any way. They can still aim to live a life of service through hospitality, self-sacrifice and charity. Other people are called to chastity. This does not devalue marriage, either. The vocation to chastity and the vocation to married life both come from God, and both should be equally valued. The two ways of life reinforce one another.

### CONTRACEPTION

The Church's teachings on contraception arise from the understanding that Catholics should only have sex within marriage and that the main function of sex is for procreation. Using contraceptives, such as a condom or the contraceptive pill, is directly against Catholic teaching. This is because these methods interfere with the natural law of God's Creation and split sex from its proper procreative role.

However, Catholics are allowed to use natural methods of birth control – chiefly by having sex only when the wife is at a low-fertility part of her cycle. Natural birth control is allowed because it is in harmony with the natural law of God's Creation and uses God-given powers, such as self-control, rather than chemical interference (as with the pill) or a physical barrier (such as a condom). Catholics must be responsible and correctly motivated in using this method: for example, it would be acceptable to use the method to space out children in a

*Above In this 14th-century detail from* The Creation of Adam *by Master Bertram of Minden, God is shown instructing Adam about his duty to procreate and father children.*

### HOMOSEXUALITY

The Church recognizes that some men and women have deep-seated homosexual tendencies: the catechism calls these tendencies "intrinsically disordered" and "contrary to natural law". Sexual relations between people of the same sex are not approved because they "close the sexual act to the gift of life" and "do not proceed from a genuine affective and sexual complementarity". The Church believes that homosexual people are called to chastity: they are required to develop self-mastery and they are expected to pray for support. In these circumstances, they can rely on God's sacramental grace to help them reach Christian perfection.

*Right Catholic parents bring their children to Christ in Lucas Cranach the Elder's* Christ Blessing the Children *(c.1540). Parents are responsible for teaching their children the Catholic faith.*

family, but to do so to avoid having children in order to have more spending money would be immoral.

The Church also teaches that sex has a unifying function – it brings the husband and wife into a close spiritual, mental and physical union. By using artificial contraception, according to the teaching, the couple are violating this function and preventing themselves from giving completely to each other.

In addition, according to the Church, the use of contraception has a number of negative effects. Among these it promotes immoral behaviour, damages marriage as an institution, makes men respect women less, and gives people the idea that they can achieve total control over bodily processes of reproduction when this control rightly belongs to God.

Opponents of the Church's position argue that contraception has benefits for people both as individuals and collectively. The Church's response is that using contraception is evil and that it is never the correct approach to do evil, even if you believe good may come of it.

## RIGHT TO LIFE

The Church takes a very strong position against the use of abortion. Catholics believe that a new life begins at the moment in which a woman's egg is fertilized by a sperm. The fertilized egg is a human being independent of mother and father. According to Pope John Paul II in his 1995 encyclical *Evangelum Vitae* ("The Gospel of Life"), abortion is

*Right The catechism teaches that God's Grace helps married couples "attain holiness in their married life and in welcoming and educating their children".*

"a grave moral disorder" because it involves the intentional killing of an innocent person. Church teaching states that every individual, including a foetus, has an inalienable right to life – and this right extends from the moment of conception until the person's physical death. In canon law, a person who procures an abortion is excommunicated.

# PENANCE AND RECONCILIATION

DURING THE SACRAMENT OF PENANCE AND RECONCILIATION, WHICH IS OFTEN REFERRED TO AS CONFESSION, CATHOLICS CONFESS ANY WRONGDOINGS TO THEIR PRIEST AND RECEIVE ABSOLUTION.

Confession provides spiritual healing for people who have been distanced from God by their sins and restores to them the Grace of God. The sacrament has two effects or aspects: outer and inner – the outer aspect is that the penitent believer receives absolution from his priest, either by remission of sin or the punishment due to sin; the inner aspect is that through repentance and confession the believer is reconciled to God.

In addition to being known as confession, penance and reconciliation can also be called the sacrament of conversion (because, according to the *Catechism of the Catholic Church*, it

***Below*** *After his Resurrection, Christ tells his disciples that they have the power to forgive sins, as seen in this 14th-century panel by Duccio di Buoninsegna.*

"makes sacramentally present Jesus' call to conversion") and the sacrament of forgiveness. Along with the anointing of the sick, confession is one of two sacraments of healing. Through these two sacraments, according to the catechism, the Church continues Christ's work of "healing and salvation, even among Her own members".

Christ instituted the sacrament of confession on Easter Day, when after rising from the dead following his Crucifixion he appeared to the apostles and said, "Receive the Holy Spirit. If you forgive the sins of any, they are forgiven; if you retain the sins of any, they are retained" (John 20:22–23).

There is another biblical precedent for this sacrament, found in the episode described in the Gospel of

***Above*** *The penitent admits any wrongdoing, but also humbly confesses (acknowledges and honours) God's profound holiness and great mercy.*

Matthew (9:2–8) in which Jesus publicly forgave the sins of a paralytic man brought to him for healing and cured him of his paralysis.

## WHEN TO CONFESS

Catholics must receive the sacrament of confession when they are aware that they have committed a mortal sin and in any case at least once a year. They are encouraged to go to confession once a month. (Mortal sins are distinct from venial sins. Mortal sins are those that condemn a soul to hell because they cannot be forgiven without repentence; lesser venial sins, if unconfessed and so not absolved, cause separation from God but not eternal damnation.)

Catholics are also required to receive the sacrament of confession before they receive the Eucharist for the first time. In Lent, the Church urges believers to receive the sacrament of confession as part of their preparation for Easter. Catholics are generally keen to receive confession

*Right Sin is straying from God, while penance, such as the confession shown in this 15th-century painting by Domenico di Niccolò dei Cori, is a return to the Father.*

because, as one of the seven sacraments instituted by Christ, it delivers God's Grace to those who receive it and so is a vital aid in living a good Christian life.

There are four key elements to the sacrament. Firstly, penitent individuals are required to be contrite; that is, to feel sincere remorse for their sins. They must have a genuine intention not to commit the sins again. Secondly, they must confess the number and kind of their sins to a priest. Thirdly, they need to receive absolution from the priest. Lastly, they must perform satisfaction or the acts of penance that were prescribed by the priest.

## ABSOLUTION FROM SIN

A priest (or bishop) does not himself have the power to forgive sins. However, he exercises the power on behalf of Christ through the sacrament of penance if he is ordained validly and has proper jurisdiction over the penitent who makes confession. In administering the sacrament, the priest acts in *persona Christi* ("in the person of Christ").

*Below In delivering absolution, a priest acts on Christ's behalf. As well as receiving God's pardon, the penitent is reconciled with the Church.*

The priest hears the confessions of his parishioners or other members of the faithful at set times, and the normal form of confession is for the penitent individual to say, "Bless me Father for I have sinned" and then to specify the period that has elapsed since his or her last confession. The penitent has to confess all mortal sins committed in that period and is encouraged to confess venial sins, too. The prayer of confession begins, "O My God I am heartily sorry…"

The priest then delivers absolution. One form describes a merciful God, who "through the death and resurrection of his Son" has become reconciled to humankind and has sent the Holy Spirit among people "for the forgiveness of sins". It goes on to state that through the Church's ministry God may pardon the person and give him or her peace. The priest ends by absolving the person from his or her sins in the three names of the Holy Trinity.

## SEAL OF THE CONFESSIONAL

The priest is bound by the absolutely inviolable seal of the confessional – he cannot reveal what he has been told in confession, even under threat of death. A priest who does so is automatically excommunicated from the Church. In criminal matters, for example, if a person admits to murder in the confessional, the priest cannot tell the police or other authorities, but he can encourage the penitent to give himself or herself up and can withhold absolution as a means of leverage.

# ANOINTING OF THE SICK AND THE LAST RITES

GOD'S GRACE IS DELIVERED TO THE SEVERELY ILL THROUGH THE ANOINTING OF THE SICK AND LAST RITES, WHICH HELP THEM COPE WITH SICKNESS OR DEATH AND RESIST THE FEELING OF DISCOURAGEMENT.

In the sacrament of the anointing of the sick, a priest anoints a seriously ill Catholic person with holy oil. Along with penance and reconciliation (or confession), the anointing of the sick is one of the Catholic Church's two sacraments of healing. Through the anointing of the sick, an ill person is united with the suffering of Christ, and even permitted to share in the redemptive work performed by Christ's Passion. The sacrament will bring spiritual and sometimes physical healing – and also forgiveness of sins.

All the sacraments draw on biblical precedent. The central text in support of the anointing of the sick is in James 5:14–15:

*Below The sacrament delivers grace to strengthen the ill person, bringing courage, peace of mind and, subject to God's will, physical healing.*

*Is any among you sick? Let him call for the elders of the Church, and let them pray over him, anointing him with oil in the name of the Lord; and the prayer of faith will save the sick man, and the Lord will raise him up; and if he has committed sins, he will be forgiven.*

## RECEIVING THE SACRAMENT

Only a priest or bishop can administer the sacrament of the anointing of the sick. According to canon law, he can give the sacrament to any member of the faithful who has reached the age of reason and is in danger of death either though illness or old age. If a person receives the sacrament when close to death, then recovers, he or she can receive this sacrament a second time if the illness strikes again. Equally, a person can receive the sacrament a second time

*Above Christ comforted and healed the sick, as illustrated by James Tissot in his 19th-century painting,* In the Villages the Sick Were Brought unto Him.

if a continuing illness worsens. A person about to have serious surgery can also receive the sacrament.

The priest can also use his pastoral judgement to determine whether or not it is appropriate to administer the sacrament a second time or even more often when a person is chronically ill or very old and weak. He can administer the sacrament to a person at home, during Mass or while in a hospital and may give it to a group of the seriously ill if desired.

## ADMINISTERING THE SACRAMENT

The priest uses olive or vegetable oil that has been blessed by the bishop in the Chrism Mass on Holy Thursday (the Thursday of Holy Week). In the Latin Rite of the Western Church, the priest usually anoints the sick person on the forehead, marking the shape of the Cross, and says: "Through this holy anointing may the Lord in his love and mercy help you with the grace of the Holy Spirit. May the

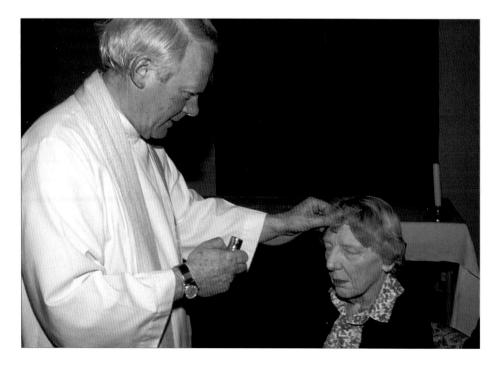

*Above A priest visiting a seriously ill person will carry all the equipment he needs to perform anointing and to celebrate the Eucharist.*

Lord who frees you from sin save you and raise you up." He may anoint other parts of the body, without using the verbal formula.

## LAST RITES

When the sick person is in immediate danger of death the anointing is considered to be one of the "last rites", which also includes penance and reconciliation and the Eucharist. The normal procedure is for the priest to hear the person's confession, then anoint him or her, before giving him or her the Eucharist. In some cases, when a person is too ill to confess, the priest can pronounce absolution – but this is believed to be effective only if the dying person inwardly feels contrition for the sins.

The Eucharist given to a seriously ill person is called *viaticum*, a Latin word meaning "provision for the voyage" and referring to the final journey of this earthly life – through death into eternal life. In the words of the *Catechism of the Catholic Church*, "As the sacrament of Christ's Passover, the

*Right In addition to anointing, those near to death confess their sins and receive the Eucharist, as in this 15th-century painting by Rogier van der Weyden.*

Eucharist should always be the last sacrament of the earthly journey, the *viaticum* for 'passing over' to eternal life." The sacrament of the anointing of the sick is also called *sacramentum exeuntium* ("the sacrament of those departing"). It is the last of the holy anointings of the Christian life, and follows on from the anointings of baptism and confirmation. "This last anointing," according to the catechism, "fortifies the end of our earthly life like a solid rampart for the final struggles before entering the Father's house."

### EXTREME UNCTION

When given among the last rites, the anointing of the sick was traditionally known as extreme unction, meaning "a last anointing". In the modern Church, the sacrament is called the anointing of the sick, but some traditional Catholics, who usually adhere to the practice and terminology in use before the Second Vatican Council (1962–5), still use the name extreme unction.

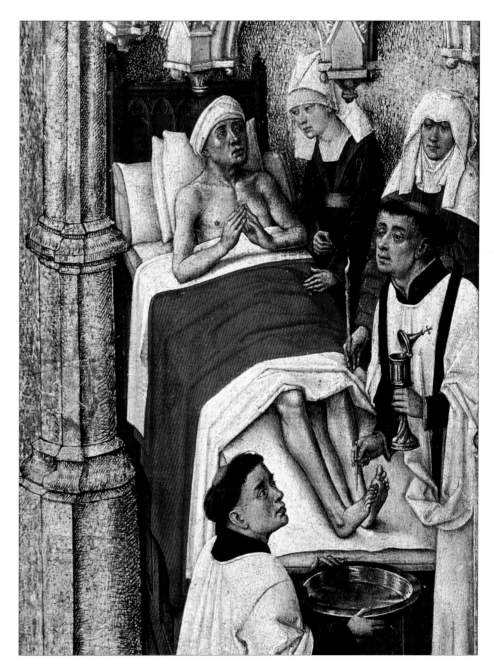

# DUST TO DUST

WHEN A PERSON DIES, CATHOLICS GIVE THANKS FOR THE GRACE OF GOD EVIDENCED IN HIS OR HER LIFE. CATHOLIC FUNERAL SERVICES COMPRISE A VIGIL, A MASS AND A BURIAL OR COMMITTAL.

The three forms of funeral service have been authorized in the *Ordo exsequiarum* ("Order of Christian Funerals") of the Catholic Church's Roman Rite. Each form has its proper place: the vigil is usually held at home; the funeral or requiem Mass in the Church; and the committal in the cemetery. All three forms express what the catechism calls the "paschal character" of death. This refers to a Catholic's understanding of death in terms of Easter, in the light of Jesus' death and Resurrection.

## VIGIL, MASS, COMMITTAL

The vigil is a gathering for prayers and biblical readings, with a sermon, that is held before the day of the funeral Mass and committal, often at the home of the deceased person. One or more eulogies on the dead person's life are shared. These should not praise the individual but concentrate on the workings of God's Grace in his or her life. The vigil is often held as part of a wake.

*Below After the funeral Mass, a priest blesses the coffin before it is transported to the cemetery for the committal.*

The funeral Mass is often called a requiem Mass. Those gathered pray for the forgiveness of sins and the salvation of the soul of the departed. The service takes the name *requiem* from the Latin wording at the beginning of the first section, the Introit: *Requiem aeternam dona eis, Domine, et lux perpetua luceat eis* ("Grant them unending rest, O Lord, and may light perpetual fall on them"). Requiem Masses can also be held as a memorial for a deceased person and to mark an anniversary of a person's death.

The rite of committal consists of prayers and Bible readings as the body is buried in a cemetery, or before cremation. In the committal the faithful bid farewell to the deceased person; the Church commends him or her to the care of God.

## FULFILMENT OF A LIFE

Catholic teaching views death as the end and fulfilment of a devout person's sacramental life. His or her religious life has been structured to lead to this end: death is the fulfilment of the new birth of baptism, of the new life that was confirmed and strengthened by the anointing

*Above During a funeral Mass, the presiding priest censes and blesses the coffin as the Church expresses its communion with the departed.*

of the Holy Spirit at confirmation, and the participation in the heavenly feast anticipated every time he or she received the Eucharist. During the funeral, the Church, which has carried the devout person through life, like a mother would care for a growing child, now offers him or her to God the Father, in Christ.

The liturgy and ceremonial of the requiem Mass generally follows that of the standard Mass, but omits its more joyful expressions, including the gloria and the Creed and certain doxologies, or hymns of praise. A key element of the Mass in this setting is the funeral homily, which must be delivered by a bishop, priest or deacon, and which explicates the meaning of death in the context of Christ's own death and his triumphant Resurrection.

Celebrating Mass is central to the funeral because the Eucharist lies at the very heart of a Catholic's understanding of death. In the Eucharist, a member of the faithful will have communion with Christ and with the departed person. The gathered faithful will then pray for the forgiveness of the deceased person's sins, and ask that he or she enjoy the heavenly feast to which the Eucharist looks forward: in doing this, and in

*Right The funeral, followed by burial or cremation, is illuminated by belief in "the resurrection of the dead, and the life of the world to come".*

receiving the Eucharist, the faithful at the Mass will learn to exist in communion with the departed.

## ATTITUDE TO CREMATION

For many centuries the Catholic Church did not allow cremation because it held the practice to be counter to belief in the resurrection of the body. The official position was that cremation was a pagan practice. However, in 1963 the Vatican began to permit the use of cremation as long as the reason for choosing it did not go against Catholic beliefs.

The initial requirement was that all funeral services had to be carried out in the presence of the dead body, which would then be cremated afterward. This was changed in 1997 and since then the funeral liturgy can be used in the presence of cremated remains of the body. The Church does not permit the scattering of ashes after cremation; it teaches that the ashes should be entombed in a grave or mausoleum.

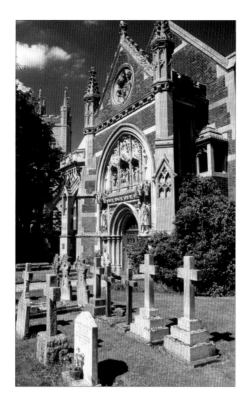

## DRESSED FOR A MASS

Bishops or priests that celebrate requiem Masses were traditionally expected to wear black vestments and ornaments. Black is considered to be the colour of the most profound grief, and is also worn for services on Good Friday. Today, clergy often wear white to symbolize the glory of the Resurrection.

## MUSICAL HERITAGE

Requiem Masses are often sung, and there is a very rich heritage of musical settings of requiem Masses, including works by the notable composers Wolfgang Amadeus Mozart, Hector Berlioz and Gabriel Fauré.

The revised form of the Latin Rite for the requiem Mass, which was introduced following the Second Vatican Council (1962–5) and is used generally today, does away with a number of elements of the traditional requiem that are familiar to people who know the service chiefly through these magnificent musical settings.

One example is the sequence beginning *Dies irae, dies illa, Solvet sæclum in favilla* ("Day of anger, day when the world turns to ashes…"). This is a powerful part of classical requiems by Mozart and Verdi, but was made optional and then dropped from the requiem Mass following the Second Vatican Council as part of changes designed to tone down elements suggestive of despair and fear of judgement while emphasizing hope and belief in the Resurrection. The *Dies irae* was part of the requiem Mass in the Roman Missal 1962 (prior to the Second Vatican Council) and so is still heard in churches that celebrate the Tridentine liturgy in use before the Council.

*Left A memorial Mass for Pope John Paul II was held in the Church of the Holy Sepulchre (the church in which Jesus is traditionally believed to be buried), in Jerusalem, on 6 April 2005. Latin Patriarch Michel Sabbah presided, and some 200 heads of state, heads of government and royalty gathered to attend the pope's funeral.*

# PRAYER

IN PRAYER, CATHOLICS CAN COMMUNICATE WITH THEIR CREATOR. BELIEVERS CAN BUILD AND MAINTAIN A LIVING AND PERSONAL RELATIONSHIP WITH GOD THE FATHER, SON AND HOLY SPIRIT.

Prayer can be public or private: it can be a shared communal experience or a personal and solitary formal rite, spoken aloud or a more fluid, silent interior activity. Public forms of prayer include the Mass and the Liturgy of the Hours. Among private forms are the use of the rosary and the practice of *Lectio Divina*, which is a meditative reading of the Scriptures developed as a form of devotion by medieval monastics. The Catholic Church teaches that the chief sources of and inspirations to prayer are the Word of God in the Bible, the liturgy of the Church and the virtues of faith, hope and charity.

## HOW TO PRAY

Catholic authorities stress that it is essential to pray but that the kind of prayer does not matter. Pope John Paul II, in writing about how to pray, said that it was a simple thing to do and recommended that you pray "any way you like, so long as you do pray". Prayer may be a very personal outpouring. The catechism quotes St Thérèse of Lisieux:

*For me prayer is a surge of the heart; it is a simple look turned towards heaven, it is a cry of recognition and of love, embracing both trial and joy.*

Prayer is not just self-expression. Elsewhere, the catechism states that prayer is not something to be turned into a "spontaneous outpouring of interior impulse". The Holy Spirit instructs the faithful in how to pray through "a living transmission" (Sacred Tradition) within the Church.

*Above In Jacob Cornelisz van Oostsanen's 1523 painting,* Adoration of the Trinity, *a Christian (right) prays with hands clasped together.*

Prayers of all kinds must be made in the name of Jesus, for these have access to God the Father through Christ. The Holy Spirit teaches believers to pray to God the Father through the Son, and that through the many different kinds of prayer the one Holy Spirit acts.

## BENEFITS OF PRAYER

The Church teaches that prayer leads the faithful away from sin toward salvation. In prayer, a believer turns to God and receives direction from the Holy Spirit; without this guidance the believer is trapped in sin. According to the Church, people who pray with eagerness and call on God cannot sin, therefore they are saved; those who do not pray are trapped in sin and are in the way of damnation.

Praying by repeating the name of Jesus in the Jesus Prayer has the effect of summoning Christ within the believer. Whereas in the Old Testament, the Jews were forbidden

### THE JESUS PRAYER

The catechism states, "There is no other way of Christian prayer than Christ." St Paul exhorted Christians to "pray constantly" (1 Thessalonians 5:17), to attempt to keep one's life in God's presence and under his eye: a favoured way of doing this is through "prayer of the heart". One example used for centuries by Christians in both the Eastern and Western Churches is the Jesus Prayer, an invocation based on repetition of the Lord's name. The Jesus Prayer developed in a variety of forms, the most common of which is "Lord Jesus Christ, Son of God, have mercy on us sinners". Praying this prayer while being active in the world sanctifies every action.

*Above Catholics are encouraged to pray in Jesus' name, who spread the Word, as shown in this 17th-century Greek icon.*

to utter the name of God, in Jesus, God adopted human form and delivered his name to humanity: the name Jesus contains the divine presence. The catechism explains: "The name 'Jesus' contains all: God and man and the whole economy of creation and salvation…whoever invokes the name of Jesus is welcoming the Son of God who loved him [or her] and who gave himself up for him [or her]."

## PRIVATE PRAYER

The Church also teaches that private meditative prayer complements and sustains the public prayer of the liturgy. In his apostolic letter *Rosarium Virginis Mariae* ("Rosary of the Virgin Mary"), which was witten on 16 October 2002, Pope John Paul II described the rosary as a good introduction and an accurate echo of Church liturgy. He added that praying the words of the rosary as taught by the Church involves carrying on an inner meditation on

the glories and hidden meanings of Christ's life and this lets the believer take part in a deep study of Christian mystery that amounts to a profound and practical training for a holy life.

*Above A prayer book, shown in this 16th-century detail from* Portrait of the Artist's Sister in the Garb of a Nun *by Sofonisba Anguissola, is an indispensable aid for some Catholics devoted to private prayer.*

Pope Benedict XVI emphasized the fact that private prayer, contemplation and religious devotions do not distract from loving service in the world but in fact provide an essential underpinning and support for that service. He used the example of Mother Teresa of Calcutta and the work of her order, the Missionaries of Charity, as an example. In his first encyclical, *Deus Caritas Est*, written in December 2005, he declared that the example of Teresa of Calcutta illustrates the fact that when we devote time to God in private or public prayer, it does not distract us from serving our neighbours in love, but rather is a limitless source of loving service.

*Left In prayer, the believer reaches out to God. The Church teaches that calling on the name of Jesus summons his presence within us.*

# THE SACRED HEART

CATHOLICS USE THE SACRED HEART OF JESUS AS A FOCUS FOR THEIR INTENSE DEVOTIONS IN WHICH THEY SEEK TO MAKE REPARATIONS TO JESUS FOR THE SINS OF HUMANKIND.

The Sacred Heart of Jesus is a symbol of God's love for humanity. God's love was expressed in Christ's suffering, and the Sacred Heart is pierced by human sins. Through prayer and contemplation, Catholics can consecrate themselves to the Sacred Heart.

In Catholic art, the Sacred Heart is usually shown to be aflame and shining with light, injured by the lance that stabbed Jesus' side on the Cross, with a crown of thorns around it and blood falling from it. This image is often superimposed on Jesus' chest, with his wounded hands pointing to the heart. The light and flames represent the power of divine love.

## DEVOTION TO THE HEART

Those who want to express their devotion to the Sacred Heart usually seek to receive Communion often. They commit to establish a "first Friday" routine – to go to confession and then receive the Eucharist on the first Friday of the month for

*Above Many Catholic homes, churches and other institutions contain Sacred Heart statues to remind the faithful of Jesus' profound love and suffering.*

nine months consecutively. They also partake of Holy Hour devotions on Thursdays. The Holy Hour is an hour-long prayer vigil, usually conducted in the presence of the Holy Sacrament. It is intended to make amends to Jesus for the hour in the garden of Gethsemane when he prayed alone, and returning to his disciples found them asleep. He reproached Peter: "So, could you not watch with me one hour? Watch and pray that you may not enter into temptation; the spirit indeed is willing, but the flesh is weak" (Matthew 26:40–41).

Sometimes the devout partake in a ceremony at home known as the enthronement of the Sacred Heart. A priest visits the home to set up ("enthrone") an image or statue of Jesus bearing his Sacred Heart: it reminds those living in the house that they have been consecrated to the Sacred Heart.

## PAPAL TEACHINGS

In his encyclical *Annum Sacrum* (On Consecration to the Sacred Heart) of 25 May 1899, Pope Leo XIII

*Below The apostles showed human frailty when they failed to keep watch with Jesus. They are asleep in Barna da Siena's 14th-century painting,* Christ in the Garden of Gethsemane.

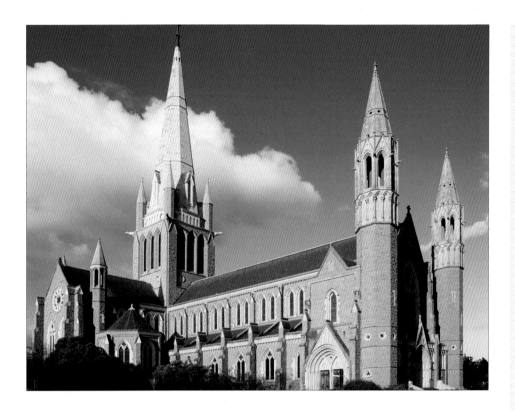

## ORIGINS OF SACRED HEART RITUALS

Medieval mystics were the first to develop the practice of revering Jesus' heart. The devotion then became popular among the Jesuits during the 16th and 17th centuries. The modern form of the devotion derives in particular from the 17th-century French mystic and nun St Marguerite Marie Alacoque, who had several revelations of the Sacred Heart in 1673–5. She declared that Jesus called on believers to offer prayers of expiation for his suffering, to take Communion frequently, especially on the first Friday of the month, and to observe the Holy Hour.

consecrated all humans to the Sacred Heart of Jesus. He described the Sacred Heart as a comprehensible symbol of Christ's endless love and declared that it was right that Catholics should dedicate themselves to the Sacred Heart; when the faithful do this, he added, they offer and bind themselves to Jesus. Many Catholic organizations, including churches, colleges and missionary and teaching orders, are dedicated to the Sacred Heart.

Pope Pius XII delivered a teaching on the mystical aspects of revering the heart of Jesus in his encyclical *Haurietis Aquas* (On Devotion to the Sacred Heart) in 1956. He declared the heart of Jesus to be a symbol of God's threefold love in the Father, Son and Holy Spirit; he wrote that believers should look devoutly upon the divine Redeemer's heart as an image of Jesus' love and a witness of our salvation in the events of Easter, and as a kind of mystical pathway along which we climb upward to be embraced by our Saviour.

Pius XII also declared in this letter that devotion to Jesus' Sacred Heart was the foundation on which

*Above The Sacred Heart Cathedral at Bendigo in Victoria, Australia, is one of many Catholic institutions named after the Sacred Heart.*

individual believers, their families and whole nations could construct the kingdom of God.

### FEAST DAY

The feast of the Sacred Heart was established in the church calendar in 1856 by Pope Pius IX and is celebrated 19 days after Pentecost. Because Pentecost falls on a Sunday, the feast of the Sacred Heart takes place on a Friday. On this feast day, devout Catholics will meditate on the devotional aspects of the Sacred Heart of Jesus.

They say the prayers laid out in the Act of Reparation to the Sacred Heart, which begins "Most sweet Jesus, whose overflowing charity for men is requited by so much forgetfulness, negligence and contempt, behold us prostrate before Thee, eager to repair by a special act of homage the cruel indifference and injuries to which Thy loving Heart is everywhere subject…"

*Above As a nun, St Marguerite Marie Alacoque had an intense mystical experience of Christ's suffering, captured in this 1888 painting,* Beatified Marguerite Marie Alacoque's Vision of Jesus' Heart, *by Antonio Ciseri.*

# STATIONS OF THE CROSS

THE STATIONS OF THE CROSS IS A SET OF 14 PENITENTIAL MEDITATIONS ON CHRIST'S PASSION, WHICH ARE OFTEN PERFORMED DURING LENT, ESPECIALLY ON FRIDAY EVENINGS.

The 14 meditations are each linked to a specific scene that illustrates one of the series of events that included Christ's condemnation to death, passage to Calvary and his Crucifixion. They are performed before paintings or statuary that represent the scene in question. The paintings or statues are usually carefully arranged around the walls of a church or chapel; however, they can also be laid out as a series of images along a pathway, for example, near a shrine.

By praying at the Stations of the Cross, the Catholic believer can make a spiritual pilgrimage. The Church teaches that the prayers and meditations before the Stations of the Cross should be performed in a spirit of reparation – in an attempt to clear away humanity's sins.

In 1928, Pope Pius XI wrote in his encyclical *Miserentissimus Redemptor* that Catholics had a duty to offer reparation to Christ for the sins that have been committed against him. In 2000, in a letter marking the 50th anniversary of the Benedictine Sisters of Reparation of the Holy Face, Pope John Paul II called the effort to make reparation for the sins committed every day against Jesus an attempt to place oneself alongside the infinite number of crosses on which the son of God is still crucified. The meditations made at these Stations often seek to focus on the positive effects of the acts of atonement that Christ performed, as well as consider the grave sins of humankind that have been the reason for Christ's suffering.

*Above* Pope John Paul II bears a cross during the first part of the Stations of the Cross in the Colosseum in Rome on 5 April 1996.

*Above* The 5th station: Jesus is judged by Pilate. These images are from a fresco by an unknown artist of the 15th century.

*Above* The 6th station: Jesus is mocked, beaten, blindfolded and crowned with thorns by enemies.

## THE OLD SEQUENCE

The traditional sequence of the Stations of the Cross was used by Catholics for centuries. It was as follows: Jesus is condemned to death (1), is given the Cross (2), then falls for the first time under the weight of the Cross (3); Jesus encounters his mother, the Blessed Virgin Mary (4), and Simon of Cyrene is forced to carry the Cross (5); Veronica (Berenice), a pious Jerusalem woman, gives Jesus her veil to wipe his face (6); Jesus falls down for a second time (7); he addresses the daughters of Jerusalem (8); he falls for a third time (9), then he is stripped of his garments (10); Jesus is nailed to the Cross (11); Jesus dies on the Cross (12); his body is removed from the Cross and laid in the arms of his mother (13), and then laid in the tomb (14).

This sequence was altered by Pope John Paul II in 1991 because the traditional sequence included six scenes (3,4,6,7,9 and 13) not backed by Scripture. The first five of these do not appear at all in biblical accounts, while station 13 – the scene of Jesus laid in his mother's arms, represented so famously and beautifully in the many Pietà statues of art history – is a misrepresentation, for in biblical accounts Joseph of Arimathea was working alone when he took down Jesus' body and laid it in a tomb.

## THE REVISED SEQUENCE

John Paul II devised a new (though not obligatory) sequence called the Scriptural Way of the Cross. The 14 scenes of this sequence are as follows: Jesus prays in the Garden of Gethsemane (1), then is betrayed by Judas Iscariot and arrested (2); he is condemned by the Jewish judicial body, the Sanhedrin (3); St Peter denies Jesus (4), then Jesus is judged by Pontius Pilate (5) and is whipped and given a crown of thorns (6); Jesus takes the Cross (7), then Simon of Cyrene carries it (8); Jesus speaks to the women of Jerusalem (9); he is crucified (10); he promises the "good thief" being crucified with him, "Truly, I say to you, today you will be with me in Paradise" (11), entrusts his mother to his disciple John with the words, "Woman, behold, your son!" and to the disciple, "Behold your mother!" (12); he dies on the Cross (13); his body is put in the tomb (14).

## GOOD FRIDAY

Catholics are generally encouraged to pray and meditate at the Stations of the Cross on Good Friday. John Paul II made a practice of performing public devotions at Stations of the Cross set up in the Colosseum, Rome, each Good Friday. In 1991 and thereafter, he prayed the new scriptural sequence outlined above. Initially, the Holy Father himself carried the Cross from station to station, but in later life his age made it necessary for him to watch the devotions from a stage while others carried the Cross. In 2007, Pope Benedict XVI approved the new sequence of the Stations of the Cross for use by Catholics.

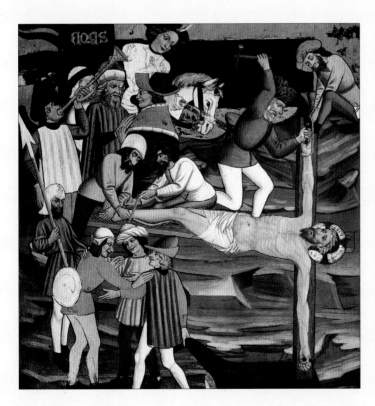

*Above* The 10th station: Jesus is bound and nailed to the Cross during his Crucifixion.

*Above* The 14th station: Jesus' body is placed in the tomb with the help of Joseph of Arimathea.

# THE ROSARY

FOR CENTURIES DEVOTED CATHOLICS HAVE USED THE ROSARY – A ROUND OF PRAYERS THAT ARE CENTRED ON THE BLESSED VIRGIN MARY – IN BOTH PUBLIC AND PRIVATE DEVOTIONS.

The rosary is also a physical object that enables believers to keep track of their prayers. It consists of a small crucifix on a circular string with a medal and a series of beads of various numbers. The beads are divided into groups of ten beads called decades, each group preceded by an individual bead set apart slightly from the others. It is used to say the prayers that form the rosary. The central prayer of the rosary is the Hail Mary:

*Hail Mary, full of Grace, the Lord is with thee; blessed art thou amongst women, and blessed is the fruit of thy womb, Jesus. Holy Mary, Mother of God, pray for us sinners now and at the hour of our death.*

The other key prayers used in the rosary to complement the Hail Mary are the Lord's Prayer beginning "Our Father, who art in Heaven…" and the Apostles' Creed beginning "I believe in God, the Father Almighty, creator of heaven and earth…"

## PRAYING THE ROSARY

The usual pattern of prayers is an introduction, then five decades of the rosary and a conclusion. During the introduction, believers hold the crucifix as they pray the dedication "In the Name of the Father, and of the Son and of the Holy Spirit: Amen" and the Apostles' Creed. Then they progress along the four beads after the crucifix, saying one Our Father and three Hail Marys.

Then they begin on the five decades. At each bead they say one Our Father and at each decade one Hail Mary. At the conclusion they hold the medal as they pray one of many other prayers to Mary, then return to the dedication "In the Name of the Father, and of the Son and of the Holy Spirit: Amen".

## THE MYSTERIES

While praying the decades of the rosary, believers meditate inwardly on the mysteries of the lives of the Virgin Mary and Jesus. These

*Above A Luminous Mystery: Peter, James and John see Jesus in his true light in Pietro Perugino's 15th–16th century* The Transfiguration.

meditations were divided into three groups of five: the Joyful Mysteries (of Jesus' birth), the Sorrowful Mysteries (of Jesus' Crucifixion) and the Glorious Mysteries (of Jesus' Resurrection). However, in 2002 Pope John Paul II proposed a new set of mysteries, the Mysteries of Light, or Luminous Mysteries, following key events in Christ's ministry.

In each group, one mystery is aligned to one decade of the rosary, so when praying the entire rosary once, believers can meditate on one set of five mysteries. There is a pattern for meditating on the mysteries: the Joyful Mysteries are considered on Monday and Saturday, the Sorrowful Mysteries on Tuesday and Friday, the Glorious Mysteries on Wednesday and Sunday and the Luminous Mysteries are optional for Thursdays.

*Left Pope John Paul II declared that the rosary prayer encompasses in its words the depth of the Holy Gospel's message.*

*Right A Glorious Mystery: The Virgin is carried to heaven and crowned in this c.1500 Flemish illustration,* Assumption and Coronation of the Virgin.

## ORIGINS AND REVIVAL

The Hail Mary is also known as the Ave Maria, which comes from its first words in Latin *Ave Maria, gratia plena, Dominus tecum.* The prayer combines three main parts, the first being the salutation delivered by the archangel Gabriel to the Blessed Virgin at the Annunciation. The second part, "Blessed is the fruit of thy womb, Jesus", derives the greeting of Elizabeth to Mary (Luke 1:42); and the third part, the prayer "Holy Mary, Mother of God…" was, according to the *Catechism of the Catholic Church,* developed by the Church.

By tradition, the rosary was developed by St Dominic when combating the heresies of the dualist Cathars in 13th-century France. It has been refined over many years, but it reached its modern form by the 15th century when the Dominican

*Below A Joyful Mystery: the Virgin Mary gives her consent to God's planned Incarnation at the Annunciation in Melchior Broederlam's 14th-century* Annunciation and Visitation.

preacher Alan de la Roche promoted its use. In 1520, Pope Leo X gave the rosary his official papal backing.

In 1858 in Lourdes, France, Marie-Bernarde Soubirous (St Bernadette) saw apparitions of the Blessed Virgin Mary, who urged her to say her rosary, and to tell others to pray, perform penances and say the rosary for the salvation of sinners. Lourdes is now a centre of pilgrimage for Catholics.

## THE WORDS OUR SAVIOUR GAVE US

Also known as the paternoster and the Our Father from its initial words in English and Latin, the Lord's Prayer is based on the one taught by Jesus to the apostles. According to the accounts in Matthew 6:9–15 and Luke 11:2–4, it runs:

*Our Father who art in heaven,*
*Hallowed be thy name.*
*Thy kingdom come,*
*Thy will be done,*
*On earth as it is in heaven.*
*Give us this day our daily bread.*
*And forgive us our trespasses,*
*As we forgive those who*
*    trespass against us.*
*And lead us not into temptation,*
*    but deliver us from evil.*

The Catholic version does not include the doxology or hymn of praise "For the kingdom the power and the glory are yours, now and forever" that appears in some other versions.

# THE BLESSING

THERE ARE CENTURIES OF TRADITION AND LAYERS OF SYMBOLISM BEHIND CATHOLIC PRACTICES, SUCH AS THE BLESSING GIVEN BY THE CLERGY, MAKING THE SIGN OF THE CROSS AND USING HOLY WATER.

When Roman Catholic priests are ordained, their hands are anointed with chrism, holy oil that has been blessed by a bishop. After receiving the sacrament of Holy Orders through this and other related rituals, priests are able to share in Christ's own priesthood: their hands have the power to bless people and objects. In the act of blessing, the clergy can sanctify both people and objects, and dedicate them to God's service.

*Above Jesus gave numerous blessings, as shown in Fernando Gallego's 15th-century* Christ Blessing, *and with a gesture of his hands worked many miracles.*

The long-held practice of sanctifying both people and objects through the act of blessing has many biblical precedents. God blessed his Creation and after the Flood blessed Noah, while priests of the Jewish faith delivered blessings on their people. Christ himself and the apostles gave blessings to the sick and needy and to their followers. The Church teaches that blessing is the chief sacramental, a rite or object through and with which the sacraments are administered.

## THE POWER TO BLESS

In general, only bishops and priests can deliver blessings, except in one exception under which a deacon is empowered to bless the paschal candle on Holy Saturday. Certain types of blessing are reserved for more senior clergy. Only the pope

*Left A stained-glass window in a Catholic church in Dublin shows a priest giving his blessing to a young child. The stained-glass windows are by the famous artist, William Early, who died during the commission.*

can deliver some blessings – for example, those to which are attached an indulgence or remission of temporal punishment due to sin.

The pope's *Urbi et Orbi* blessing to the city of Rome and to the world, which is delivered every year on Easter and Christmas, has an indulgence attached for all Catholics who hear it in person, on television or on radio. Only bishops can deliver another class of blessings – for example, blessings on churches, cemeteries, chalices and vestments.

## PRIESTLY BLESSINGS

There is a wide range of blessings that can be made by priests. They include blessings for the sick or for women due to deliver a baby and for people at various stages of Church life. There are also blessings for sanctifying objects used in religious devotions, such as crosses, images of Jesus, bells,

*Above Pope Benedict XVI delivers the papal* Urbi et Orbi *blessing. He prays that God's blessing should settle on the listening faithful and be with them always.*

medals, candles, rosaries and so forth. There are blessings for animals, food, buildings, such as schools or hospitals, and public objects, such as bridges, ships, stores, planes and so on.

The Church teaches that blessing is necessary and efficacious because people, animals and objects are all part of the Creation touched by sin after the Fall and therefore vulnerable to evil spirits. The blessings counter this effect by invoking the name of God, Father, Son and Holy Spirit and usually also by using the sign of the cross, a symbol of God's mercy and of Christ's victory over sin.

## THE SIGN OF THE CROSS

When Catholics make the sign of the cross, they are honouring the Cross of Calvary and the redemptive sacrifice of Jesus. The Cross is a symbol of both God's mercy and his victory through Christ over sin.

Individual believers make the sign of the Cross on their own bodies as an expression of devotion. The most common form is to touch forehead, breastbone or stomach, left shoulder and then right shoulder in sequence. Usually the believer prays "In the Name of the Father" when touching the forehead, "And of the Son" when touching the stomach, "And of the Holy Spirit" when touching the left and right shoulders in sequence.

## HOLY WATER

Sometimes a person will touch his fingers in holy water before making the sign of the Cross. When the faithful arrive at church for Mass, they dip their fingers in the bowl of holy water that is kept in a font near the entrance and make the sign of the Cross on head and torso.

The holy water has been blessed by a priest, and in this action the faithful bring to mind their baptismal promises as they seek to purify themselves before preparing to receive the Eucharist. Holy water is sometimes used to bless the faithful by sprinkling them with an aspergil (silver water sprinkler) during the Mass, especially during the Easter season. It is also used in blessings to sanctify places, objects and people.

## DIMINUTIVE CROSSES

A variant form of the ritual is to use the thumb to make a small sign of the Cross three times over forehead, lips and chest, sometimes while praying quietly "May Christ's words be in my mind, on my lips and in my heart". This is the normal usage when the gospel is proclaimed during Mass. A third kind of Cross made by the clergy is a small sign, traced with the thumb, for example, on the forehead of a baby in the sacrament of baptism or on the Holy Gospel during the liturgy of the Word in the Mass.

*Above A priest makes the sign of the Cross on a child's forehead using his thumb. The sign assures the child of God's protection.*

# THE CATHOLIC YEAR

The Catholic liturgical year has been shaped by events in the life of Christ. Although the actual historical dates of these events are uncertain, over the centuries a chronology has evolved that reflects the principal milestones of Christ's life as described in the Scriptures. However, at the same time it considers the manner in which human progress through time has fluctuated with the seasonal cycles. Thus "Christ our Light" was born after the deep night of the winter solstice, and our redemption from despair and damnation came in spring, after the full moon of the equinox. In the Catholic calendar, these natural cycles have assumed a religious dimension as they are allied to the life of the God-man who Catholics believe died for humankind's eternal salvation.

Just as in the life of each individual, "ordinary time" is also a component of the liturgical year. During ordinary time, no specific events in Christ's life are celebrated, although holy days of obligation such as All Saints' and the Assumption of Mary do fall within ordinary time. Strictly speaking, "ordinary" here refers to ordinal, or numbered, time; it encompasses the period from the evening of Candlemas (2 February) until Shrove Tuesday, and again from the Monday after Pentecost until vespers the night before Advent. Ordinary time pays homage to the simpler days that Christ spent on earth and reminds us to consider, even now, how we go about our normal daily lives.

*Above* Mary presides over ranks of saints in this fresco in the baptistery dome of Padua Cathedral, with her eminence emphasized by an enveloping golden aureole.

*Left* Youthful Christians bear a massive wooden cross in Jerusalem's Church of the Holy Sepulchre, built at the site of Christ's Crucifixion. The original 4th-century church was built by Constantine; the present structure dates from the Crusades of the 12th century.

# HOLY DAYS

ROMAN CATHOLICS CONSECRATE EACH DAY OF THE YEAR TO REMEMBRANCE OF AN EVENT IN THE LIFE OF CHRIST OR THE BLESSED MOTHER, OR TO ONE OF THE SAINTS.

There are around 10,000 Catholic saints, and in the Catholic year, which is known as the liturgical year, each day has some sacred significance relating to a saint. Catholics nourish their spiritual consciousness by meditating on the particular virtues and mysteries that are invoked by the history of the saint on each new feast or saint's day.

### THE FIRST HOLY DAYS

The tradition of saints' days dates back to the first centuries of the Catholic Church during the Roman persecutions. The first saints were the Christian martyrs, and early Christians often honoured their sacrifice by celebrating the day of their death, also known as their "birthday into heaven". During the Middle Ages, saints' days were a common method of dating, so "St Martin's Tide", or "Martinmas", referred to a date near 11 November, the feast day of St Martin of Tours; "Bartholomew Tide" meant a date

*Below Farm labourers, such as the one in this 15th-century image from the* Historia Naturalis, *often stopped working on the many holy days in medieval times, so holy days were unpopular among landowners.*

in the waning days of summer, on about 24 August (commemorating St Bartholomew, patron of printers).

The Church classifies the daily liturgical observations as solemnities, feasts, memorials and commemorations. Solemnities, as their name implies, are the most important, but of the 13 yearly solemnities, only 6 are classified as holy days of obligation in the United States and 10 in Europe. (This group of six does not include ordinary Sundays, when Catholics are obliged to attend Mass each week, in honour of the day Christ rose from the dead.)

The Catholic Church mandates that Catholics must attend Mass on holy days of obligation, and refrain from "unnecessary servile work", often defined as physical labour. This prohibition is the genesis of today's word "holiday", which is an obvious contraction of "holy day". In feudal times serfs were freed on holy days of obligation so they could attend Mass.

### MEDIEVAL HOLY DAYS

By the Middle Ages, holy days were so numerous and engrained in the observances of society that in some quarters they came to be considered a nuisance. The prohibition against servile work was taken up by the populace with enthusiasm, and soon medieval lawmakers found themselves having to issue stern decrees to make "exemptions" from the command not to work on holy days so that crucial work, such as harvesting, did not come to a standstill. The *Catholic Encyclopedia* notes that from the 13th to the 18th century, some dioceses observed more than 100 feast days – days in which no work was done. Celebrations of the

*Above St Bartholomew is associated with books, as in this 14th-century illustration by Andre Beauneveu, because of a printers' celebration, the Wayzgoose. It is held on 24 August, the time of year printers began to work by candlelight.*

"octaves" of major Catholic holy days, such as Easter, could cause work to stop for more than a week. Complaints reached a crescendo in the 16th century, and finally in 1642 Pope Urban VIII bowed to the inevitable and issued an encyclical, *Universa per Orbem*, that reduced the number of holy days to 36 (not including Sundays).

Even priests are subject to normal human nature, and in 1858 Pope Pius IX had to issue a second encyclical – this time to order priests to offer Mass on the "suppressed" holy days. This was issued because some priests had decided to take a holiday of their own and had ceased to celebrate Mass on feasts that were no longer holy days of obligation, although to do so was still their responsibility.

## EUROPEAN HOLY DAYS

Holy days of obligation vary from country to country and year to year. In Europe, holy days are often celebrated with opulence. In Rome, for example, the Feast of Sts Peter and Paul (29 June) is a general holiday for the entire city, marking the day in AD 64 when both saints were martyred for their faith (Peter by being crucified upside down and Paul by beheading). Today, Romans observe the holy day with extravagant decoration of the 4th-century basilicas dedicated to each saint, and each year the pope presents palliums (from the Latin for "stole") to the city's bishops. The palliums are newly woven from wool shorn from lambs, and they symbolize the lamb carried over the shoulders of the good shepherd, reminding the bishops they are the shepherds of their pastoral flock, just as was Peter, Rome's first bishop.

## AMERICAN HOLY DAYS

The holy days of obligation in the USA are fewer than in Europe. This is, in part, because the tradition of their celebration is shorter than in many European countries, where Catholicism has been the majority religion for many centuries. In the early years of the United States,

Catholics were a minority, widely scattered in a vast country, and victims of prejudice. Puritans did not celebrate holy days because they had been offended by the excesses that they had observed in Europe. American bishops took such realities into account and reduced the number of holy days.

In the United States, if All Saints' Day or Ascension falls on a Saturday or Monday, the obligation to attend Mass is rescinded. The American Conference of Bishops has also suppressed certain holy days that are still active in Europe: the observances for Epiphany (6 January), Corpus Christi (the Thursday after Trinity Sunday), St Joseph (19 March) and the apostles Sts Peter and Paul (29 June) have been moved to the next following Sundays.

American holy days of obligation, with the exception of Christmas, are normally celebrated in a low-key manner simply by going to Mass. However, in certain American ethnic enclaves, old traditions of celebration on a saint's day still endure; for example, the feast of San Gennaro is usually celebrated with a street fair in Manhattan's Little Italy.

*Above On the feast of Sts Peter and Paul in Rome, Pope Benedict XVI drapes a pallium made of new woven wool over the shoulders of an archbishop.*

*Below The September feast of San Gennaro, here celebrated in New York's Little Italy neighbourhood, home of many Italian-Americans, honours the 4th-century martyrdom of Januarius, the patron saint of Naples.*

# THE FESTIVE CALENDAR

THE FEASTS OF THE CATHOLIC CALENDAR HAVE MARKED THE DAYS OF THE YEAR FOR CENTURIES. SOME FEASTS OCCUR ON THE SAME DAY EACH YEAR, BUT OTHERS MOVE DEPENDING ON THE LUNAR CYCLE.

Like the saints that they honour, Catholic feast days have been ranked and classified. Solemnity is the highest ranking of the holy days, but depending on the country it is not always a holy day of obligation. A feast day is the next highest rank of holy days, with celebrations that honour Jesus, Mary and the saints. A memorial is the lowest rank of holy days, a way of honouring saints without giving them fully fledged feast days. Below is a key to symbols that indicate if the feast has a fixed or moveable date, and when a day of obligation is celebrated by most countries or only those in Europe.

KEY
† moveable feast
z fixed feast
i Holy Day of Obligation
v Additional European Holy Day of Obligation

*Above A calendar of saints' days from a 14th-century French Bible highlights the numerous days that were celebrated.*

*Left St Paul's conversion to Christianity, captured in this 15th-century painting by Hildesheim, is celebrated on 25 January.*

## JANUARY
1   Solemnity of Mary Mother of God   z   i
6   Solemnity of Epiphany   z   v
13   Feast of Baptism of Jesus   z
25   Feast of the Conversion of St Paul   z

## FEBRUARY
2   Feast of Candlemas (Presentation)   †   z
5   Shrove Tuesday   †
6   Ash Wednesday   †

## MARCH
2   Laetare Sunday   †
16   Palm Sunday   †
19   Spy Wednesday   †
19   St Joseph   †
20   Maundy Thursday   †
21   Good Friday   †
23   Easter   †
25   Solemnity of the Annunciation   z

*Above Many feast days celebrate Jesus and the Virgin Mary, depicted together in this Byzantine painting.*

## MAY
*1* Ascension † i
*11* Pentecost †
*18* Feast of Trinity Sunday †
*22* Solemnity of Corpus Christi
    † v
*30* Sacred Heart of Jesus †
*31* Immaculate Heart of Mary †

*Above In Valencia, Spain, the feast of Corpus Christi is marked with processions of* rocas, *carts decorated with holy statues.*

## JUNE
*29* Solemnity of Sts Peter and
    Paul v

## AUGUST
*15* Solemnity of Assumption
    of Mary z i

## SEPTEMBER
*18* Birth of the Virgin Mary z
*29* Mass of archangels Michael,
    Raphael and Gabriel z

## NOVEMBER
*1* All Saints' Day z i
*2* All Souls' Day z
*23* Feast of Christ the
    King z
*30* First Sunday of Advent †

## DECEMBER
*7* Second Sunday of Advent †
*8* Feast of the Immaculate
    Conception z i
*14* Gaudete Sunday (Third
    Sunday of Advent) †
*21* Fourth Sunday of
    Advent †
*25* Christmas Day z i
*28* Solemnity of the Holy
    Family †

*Above The holy days of All Saints and All Souls are celebrated in Mexico with graveside offerings, including* pan de muertos *– bread made for the dead.*

*Above Michael, Raphael and Gabriel, the only archangels in the Scriptures, share a feast day in September. They are shown in this 15th-century image by Domenico di Michelino with Tobias, an encounter described in the* Book of Tobit.

*Left Christmas in midwinter, lights against the darkness – despite the debate and uncertainty about the true date of Christ's birth, it is celebrated around the world on 25 December.*

# A CHILD IS BORN

CHRISTMAS, A SEASON THAT CATHOLICS DEVOTE TO THE CELEBRATION OF JESUS' BIRTH, ENCOMPASSES TWO PERIODS IN THE CATHOLIC CHURCH: ADVENT AND CHRISTMASTIDE.

Advent is a season of preparation that is about four weeks long, although it is sometimes a little shorter, depending on the day of the week the 25th falls on. It will always include four Sundays. Christmastide is the period from Christmas Day to the feast of the Epiphany on 6 January – the traditional 12 days of Christmas.

## CELEBRATING ADVENT

Like the secular Christmas, the Catholic Christmas (from Old English *Cristes Maesse*, or "Mass of Christ") involves weeks of preparation. However, unlike the frenzied weeks of shopping promoted by the worldly media, the four weeks of Advent (from the Latin *Adventus*, or

*Above The Magi, probably Persian kings, visited Christ when he was nearly a year old – not in the stable, as some traditions suggest. Gerard David captured the visit in his* Adoration of the Kings, *c.1515.*
.

"coming") involve steady spiritual preparation, marked by a certain amount of sober sacrifice and longing in the beginning, but as Christmas Day approaches, a mounting sense of joy. On the third Sunday of Advent, known as Gaudete (or "Rejoice") Sunday, the heightened anticipation is symbolized by a change in the colour of the priest's vestments from purple to rose.

Celebration of Advent originated in the 5th century, when Bishop Perpetuus of Tours decreed a fast, known as "St Martin's Lent", from St Martin's Day (11 November) to Christmas. In the 6th century, Pope Gregory the Great shortened Advent to four weeks, its modern duration, and strict fasting gave way to a less rigorous abstinence from meat and dairy. The liturgy of Advent emphasizes that preparation for Christ's first coming at his birth prefigures the preparations that Christians should make for his Second Coming.

## THE NATIVITY

One of the most widely known and beloved stories is that of Christ's Nativity. The tradition of the divine birth in a primitive stable in the

## DOMESTIC RITUALS

The domestic rituals of Advent evolved as expressions of the longing and expectation that characterize the season. The colourful family ceremonies are particularly attractive to children, helping them to focus on the spiritual rather than the commercial meaning of the season. The Advent wreath is a circular wreath of evergreens with four evenly spaced candles, three violet and one rose, to represent the four weeks of Advent. The violet symbolizes penitence, and the rose, lit on the third Sunday known as Gaudete Sunday, represents joy at the imminent approach of the Nativity. Families gather at a weekly Sunday dinner to light the candles, a new candle as each week passes, and dine by their light in the December evening. Some modern wreaths also include a white candle, symbolic of Jesus, that is lit on Christmas Eve. The familial ritual reminds Catholics of the intimate scene of the Holy Family within the snug stable.

Nativity scenes are usually small enough to fit on a table or mantelpiece. Some are simple and homemade, others are heirloom sets crafted by old world-artisans. The stable, the barn animals and the manger are arranged before Christmas, and Mary and Joseph are allowed to set up housekeeping, but the infant Jesus and the Magi must await the day appointed for their arrival in Scripture. Meanwhile, each day children add a few wisps of straw to the manger. By Christmas Eve, the manger will be comfortable for the infant figure, who arrives on time and with

ceremony – gently placed in the manger at midnight on Christmas Eve. On Epiphany, the royal visitors from the East arrive, and the three kings are added to the stable scene.

*Right The weekly ritual of lighting the Advent wreath in church or at home helps children understand the spiritual significance of the Advent season.*

*Right* *Although born in a humble setting,*
*the Christ child seems to transfix the gaze*
*of all in this 15th-century illustration by*
*Rosello Franchi and Filippo Torelli.*

depth of winter concentrates the
sense of mystery and delight that
Catholics experience during this
season. However, despite the hold
that the Nativity story has on the
popular imagination, the date of
Jesus' birth is still unknown, and the
only gospel to describe the Nativity
is Luke, Chapter 2, in just a few words
that have echoed down the centuries:

> *And she brought forth her first*
> *born son and wrapped him in*
> *swaddling clothes and laid him*
> *in a manger: because there was no*
> *room for them in the inn.*

Around this quiet description,
combined with the telling in
Matthew, Chapter 2 of the wise men
from the East who saw the star of the
King of the Jews and travelled to seek
and adore him, has arisen the vast
tradition of the Christian Nativity in
story and especially in art.

## A DATE IN QUESTION

In the early centuries of the Church,
Christmas was not celebrated; some
early theologians, such as Origen
(AD 185–254), viewed celebrating
the birthday of Christ with disfavour,
calling it a pagan custom. The actual
date of Christ's birth was also much
disputed. Scriptural evidence for the
date of the Nativity is inconclusive,
and many scholars have argued that
shepherds would not have kept their
flocks in the fields at night in winter.
The choice of 25 December was a
compromise. Because the Church
identified Christ with the coming of
the light of redemption, it seemed
most natural to celebrate the birth of
"Christ Our Light" at a time when
light was reborn after the solstice on
21 December. The date also takes
advantage of a deep-rooted human

urge to celebrate at this time; the
Roman holiday of *Sol Invictus*, or
the birth of the Unconquered Sun,
and the birthday of Mithras, the
Persian God of Light, were both
celebrated in December. By the 4th
century, Christ's birth was celebrated
in Rome on 25 December; early
celebrations of Christmas were often
combined with the older celebrations
of Epiphany on 6 January.

*Right* *The birth of Christ Our Light, after*
*the winter solstice, reached its fruition at the*
*Transfiguration, when Christ shone before*
*his apostles. Fra Angelico painted the scene*
*in* The Transfiguration, *1436–45.*

# CARNIVAL!

THE MOST JUBILANT OF ALL OF THE CATHOLIC FESTIVALS, CARNIVAL IS INEXTRICABLY LINKED TO LENT, THE MOST AUSTERE. CARNIVAL HAS BEEN CELEBRATED BY CATHOLICS FOR SEVERAL CENTURIES.

As the predecessor to Lent in Catholic countries, carnival is a riotous indulgence of role reversal and licentious behaviour that has occurred for centuries. The word "carnival" probably derives from the medieval Latin phrase *carnem levare*, meaning "to remove meat". The linking of carnival and Lent in the calendar expresses an apparently innate human desire for cycles of feast and famine.

Some historians suggest that the Catholic Church was aware that carnival, which originated in southern European countries, was simply the ancient Roman pagan festival of Saturnalia under another name, yet tolerated the festival in order to smooth the transition from old pagan observances to those of the new religion. However, it is also true that the Catholic Church, especially when compared to the more sober Christian sects, such as Puritans or Quakers, has always had an appreciation of festival and pageantry.

## EARLY CELEBRATIONS

Contemporary carnivals are often associated with Rio de Janeiro – which mixes the European tradition with native American and African cultures: Venice, New Orleans and the Caribbean – and they almost always include vast costume parades with elaborate floats. However, carnival celebrations in Catholic countries have a long history – the Venetian carnival is mentioned in documents from 1092. In ancient times, carnival is said to have begun just after Epiphany (6 January) and lasted until Shrove Tuesday (*see* Shrove Tuesday, *below*), but in Rome the carnival was permitted to last for eight days, from the Monday of the week before Lent until Shrove Tuesday.

*Above Like carnival, the Roman festival of Saturnalia was officially approved and served as an antidote to a more solemn time – Saturnalia was held in mid-winter; and carnival before Lent.*

## THE POPE AND CARNIVAL

Right up through the 19th century, Rome held a famous carnival that was supported, sometimes implicitly and sometimes explicitly, by the popes. No Roman carnival could begin without a papal edict, and depending on the reigning pope, that edict might be withheld.

Some popes, such as the 15th-century Pope Paul II, were involved in planning for carnival. Paul II ordered the Jewish people of Rome to pay a yearly tax of 1,130 gold

## SHROVE TUESDAY

The British version of carnival, which is held on the day before the first day of Lent, is Shrove Tuesday. It takes its name from the verb "to shrive", meaning to absolve of sin and give penance. Medieval custom was to confess and receive penance just before Lent in order to approach the austere week in a state of penitent purity.

A more whimsical name for Shrove Tuesday is Pancake Day because fasting was practised during Lent, and pancakes were a convenient way to use up any remaining eggs, milk and butter. This particular Tuesday has many aliases and is also known as Mardi Gras, which is French for another common name, Fat Tuesday. New Orleans is renowned for its Mardi Gras, its carnival celebrations that culminate on Fat Tuesday.

*Right A 19th-century vignette by Basile de Loose shows the making of pancakes, enjoyed by young and old.*

*Above The pre-Lenten celebration of carnival reaches its apotheosis in Rio de Janeiro's sambodrome, a custom-built parade ground for carnival extravaganzas.*

florins (the 30 added to recall Judas and the 30 pieces of silver), and the money was spent on carnival. Paul II also paid, straight from the papal treasury, for races for the elderly, children, asses and bulls. Conversely, Pope Sixtus V (elected in 1585) directed that gibbets and whipping posts be erected on the piazzas as a warning not to let carnival licentiousness to verge to the criminal.

In the 16th century, the Church attempted to steal carnival's thunder by holding a 40-hour prayer service on Monday and Shrove Tuesday – however, the 40 hours of prayer did not have a lasting negative effect on carnival's popularity.

## RACES AND CANDLES

The high points of the Roman carnival, popular from the 17th century onward, were the race of Berber horses and the Race of the Candles, both held in the Via del Corso. The riderless horses were released, wearing balls full of sharp pins hanging from their sides to goad them on down the crowded Corso. In 1882, 15 people were killed when the horses charged into the crowd, and that put an end to this tradition.

The Festa dei Moccoletti (candles) was held on the last night of carnival, when the people dressed in costume, and carrying candles and lanterns, swarmed through the streets trying to put out others' candles while keeping their own lit. The custom also ended in the 19th century, but children in Rome still celebrate it by going to school in costume.

*Above The Race of the Candles involved three wooden pillars – representing Sts George, Ubaldo and Anthony – raced to the basilica. They seem ready to topple in this 19th-century Italian illustration.*

# ASH WEDNESDAY AND LENT

LENT IS AN AUSTERE PERIOD OF SPIRITUAL PREPARATION LEADING UP TO EASTER. IT STARTS ON ASH WEDNESDAY, AND DEVOUT CATHOLICS FAST DURING THIS 40-DAY PERIOD.

Lent is a period of penitence and self-denial. It developed as an adaptation of an ascetic period of study and prayer followed by early postulants converting to Christianity. They undertook this period before being baptized on Easter eve. Pre-baptism instruction in these early centuries also included exorcism; descriptions of such initiation preparations are found in the 3rd-century *Apostolic Tradition*, a written collection of early Christian practices attributed to St Hippolytus. The word "Lent" derives from Middle English *Lenten*, or "spring", and is related to the German root for "long", because the days in spring get longer.

*Below A 16th-century Flemish artist has portrayed carnival as a corpulent figure among revellers. He is armed with a spitted fowl, ready to do battle with the opposing force of Lent, who thrusts a baker's paddle bearing fish toward him.*

## THE PERIOD OF LENT

Lent lasts for a total of 40 days, in imitation of the number of days Christ was in the wilderness, fasting and withstanding the temptations of Satan (Matthew 4:1–2, Mark I:12–13, Luke 4:1–2). Until the 600s, Lent always began on Quadragesima Sunday, 40 days before Easter, but Pope Gregory the Great moved the start to Ash Wednesday to achieve 40 days without counting Sundays, which are feast days, when fasting is relaxed. During Lent, fasting was general: law courts were closed (in AD 380, the Roman emperor Gratian decreed that all legal proceedings be suspended for 40 days); theatres were shuttered; and hunting and military manoeuvres were all forbidden.

## THE START OF LENT

On Ash Wednesday, priests smear the foreheads of penitents with ash (made by burning the palms used in

*Above Jesus' 40-day fast in the desert, when he was tempted by the devil, is captured in this 19th-century painting by Ivan Nikolaevich Kramskoy. It is the model for the 40-day period of Lent.*

the previous year's Palm Sunday celebration) in the shape of a cross, saying "Remember that you are dust, and to dust you shall return" (Genesis 3:19), a reminder to those who have revelled in the excesses of Mardi Gras. Expressing penitence by using ashes is a custom inherited from ancient Jewish observance. In the Old Testament, Job expresses penitence to God with the words, "Therefore I despise myself and repent in dust and ashes" (Job 42:6).

*Right Lent's sobriety is represented by this stark composition of ash and palm, invoking the two celebrations of Ash Wednesday and Palm Sunday.*

In the early days of Christianity, ashes were used for those who had declared serious sins and asked to be shriven; the penance imposed began on Ash Wednesday and exiled the penitents from society for the 40 days of Lent; this custom is the genesis of the word "quarantine". The ashes were not smeared in a cross but sprinkled on the heads of the sinners. Over time, a public display of humility and penitence by the mark of the ashen cross became widespread.

## FASTING DURING LENT

Lent has always been associated with fasting; there is a scriptural basis for this, as in Matthew 9:15, Christ, when questioned why his disciples, unlike the Pharisees, did not fast, commented, "Days will come, when the bridegroom shall be taken away from them, and then they shall fast." It was after Jesus' departure that Christians began fasting. By the 12th century, St Bernard of Clairvaux noted that Lenten fasting was general: "kings, and princes, clergy and laity…" all fasted. When King Wenceslaus of Bohemia needed to eat meat during Lent due to ill health, he first sought dispensation from the pope. The "Black Fast" referred to one meal, taken in the evening, consisting of bread, herbs and water. Rules for fasting have become more lenient over time, but devout Catholics will still fast on Lenten Fridays.

## MODERN FASTING

For today's Catholics, 40 days of Lenten fasting in imitation of Christ's trial and temptation in the wilderness can be a particularly instructive experience, as we are so accustomed to relative plenty. A strict fast today is defined as only one meal, with two smaller meals that taken together would not equal a full meal. Animal foods, except fish, are avoided. As Christ lay in the tomb for 40 hours, the devout undertake a total fast for 40 hours just prior to Easter.

Catholics often undertake fasting as a family affair (although children under 14, according to canon law, are not required to fast), with the entire family choosing to give up meat, dessert, television or video games, then donating the money saved by this abstinence to charity, following the ancient Lenten tradition of almsgiving. Catholics are also encouraged to allow a sort of spiritual plenty to fill the space no longer occupied by temporal delights – Lent is a time of prayer and meditation. For this little time, Catholics follow the rigorous practice of monks, hoping to achieve some of the same religious insight.

Participating in fasting and other forms of abstinence are understood to be physical self-control that mirrors spiritual discipline. The Catholic catechism describes fasting as an "interior penance" and "spiritual preparation" that prepares Catholics for the arrival of Christ in the Eucharist, at his Resurrection and at the Second Coming.

*Below On Ash Wednesday, the first of Lent's 40 days, Catholics wear a cross of ash on the forehead, a symbol of penitence since Old Testament times.*

# HOLY WEEK

THE WEEK LEADING UP TO EASTER IS A PERIOD IN WHICH CATHOLICS REMEMBER AND MOURN THE SUFFERING OF JESUS, WHEN HE WAS SACRIFICED ON THE CROSS TO REDEEM HUMANKIND.

The week before Easter begins with Palm Sunday and extends to the vigil of Easter at sunset on Holy Saturday; it is known as Holy Week. During Holy Week devout Catholics follow along with Christ in a respectful attempt to take on the burden of the agony that he accepted as the price for their redemption.

Before the agony in the garden, anticipating the trial about to come, Christ said to Peter and the sons of Zebedee, "I am sorrowful even unto death….Stay you here and watch with me" (Matthew 26:38). The apostles, though, fell asleep, leaving Christ alone; he reproached them with, "Could you not watch one hour with me?" (Matthew 26:40). The liturgy and customs of Holy Week draw Catholics along with Christ's Passion, so that they "watch" with Christ and try to make reparation for that original abandonment.

## IN MOURNING

The stark and mournful tone of Holy Week is marked in many churches by obscuring all statues and crucifixes in purple veiling. The custom derives from the European tradition of hiding the altar crucifix behind a

*Above Judas was paid 30 pieces of silver to betray Christ. He is shown with the apostles' money bag in this 16th-century fresco by Eglise St Sébastien Plampinet.*

hanging that would be dropped to the ground during Palm Sunday, and reading from Matthew 27:51: "And behold the veil of the temple was rent in two from the top even to the bottom." This was one of the cataclysms that followed Christ's death. The liturgical atmosphere is of a community in mourning: the altar is not decorated with flowers, and the Te Deum and gloria are not sung.

## FROM PALM SUNDAY

In Scripture, Holy Week begins with the entry of Jesus into Jerusalem, his way strewn with palms and lauded with the Hosannas of the multitude, an event described by all four Evangelists. However, the triumph was short-lived; by Friday, Jesus would hang from the Cross. Today the entry into Jerusalem is commemorated as Palm Sunday. Palms are distributed at Mass, and some palms are saved to burn to make ashes for the next year's Ash Wednesday, symbolically linking

*Left After the Last Supper, Christ washed the apostles' feet. The ritual of washing feet, shown in Giovanni Agostino da Lodi's painting, 1500, symbolizes repentance.*

triumph (palms) and penitence and death (ash). Wednesday of Holy Week is also known as "Spy Wednesday", referring to Judas and his agreement to betray Christ for 30 pieces of silver.

## THE HEART OF THE WEEK

Easter Triduum (*triduum* is Latin for "three days") refers to the three days at the heart of Holy Week: Maundy Thursday, Good Friday and Holy Saturday. In Anglo-Saxon times, the Triduum was called "The Still Days", referring to the sorrow Catholics feel at this time, as well as to the time Christ lay in the tomb.

Maundy Thursday has tremendous significance for the Catholic Church, because it is on this day, at the paschal meal of the Last Supper, that Christ instituted the Eucharist. "Maundy" from the Latin *Mandatum*, or "commandment", refers to Christ's injunction to the apostles at the Last Supper, "A new commandment I give unto you, That ye love one another; as I have loved you" (John 13:34).

In John's Gospel, there is also a description of Christ humbly washing the apostles' feet on this day, and some churches commemorate Holy Thursday by a ritual in which the diocesan bishop washes the feet of 12 parishioners. In monasteries, the tradition was for the abbot to wash the feet of an ordinary monk.

After Thursday evening Mass, known as the Mass of the Lord's Supper, the altar is stripped of all cloths and candles, and the Eucharist in its chalice is removed from the tabernacle on the central altar and set in an unobtrusive side altar, known as the "altar of repose". The central altar remains bare and desolate of the sacred presence for all of Good Friday, the day marking Christ's Crucifixion and his death. Many churches remain open so that their parishioners can stay and pray quietly, "watching" with Christ in his time of need.

*Above A cross is borne through the streets in Corsica, France, on Good Friday.*

No masses are celebrated on Good Friday – the only day of the liturgical year on which it is forbidden to celebrate the Mass. Good Friday observances often include the Way of the Cross. Parishioners and clergy assemble in the late afternoon (Scripture notes that Christ died at the ninth hour, or 3 p.m.) at some public meeting place outdoors and carry a large cross in procession through the streets, stopping at designated points along the route to recite the Stations of the Cross. This public ritual is another example of the effort Catholics make during Holy Week to share and make reparation for the agony that Christ experienced for their sake.

## THE TENEBRAE SERVICE

Although the events commemorated by Holy Week occurred around 2,000 years ago, the Tenebrae is designed to help Catholics bridge the emotional distance and experience Christ's Passion as though they were there. "Tenebrae" means "shadows or darkness", and the service makes its participants feel as though a dark cloud has just passed over the sun.

The elements of the Tenebrae date from the 5th century. The original Tenebrae services were held in monasteries in the earliest morning hours. Today the service is held on either Maundy Thursday or Good Friday, usually at dusk. The church is in semi-darkness, the only light source a triangular candelabra known as the hearse, from the Middle English *herse*, or "harrow" (the two were similar in shape). As the service of sorrowful psalms, chants and lamentations is read, the candles are extinguished one by one until only a single lit candle remains. Then the celebrants, making no sound, leave the altar, marooning the congregation in the dark, silent church. Suddenly, a rough, clattering noise, known as the *strepitus* (Latin for "wild din" or "crash") is heard. It represents the convulsion of the earth at Christ's death. The congregation file from the church in silence, their way lit only by a few candles as they depart.

*Right Since the 13th century, the hearse has held candles during the Tenebrae service. "Hearse" later came to refer to a candle frame over a coffin, and from that to the vehicle that carries a coffin.*

# THE RESURRECTION AND EASTER

AFTER THE SOMBRE HOLY WEEK, CATHOLICS AROUND THE WORLD CELEBRATE EASTER, A JOYOUS OCCASION COMMEMORATING THE RESURRECTION OF CHRIST OUR LIGHT.

To Catholics, Easter is the greatest Catholic celebration and completes the meaning of all that came before and all that followed and is to come in Christian history. Without Easter, Catholic doctrine has no point, but all of Christianity is enlivened by the Resurrection of Christ on Easter.

The name "Easter" in Germanic languages is derived from old English and Germanic root words referring to the East and dawn. *Eastre* or *Ostara* was also the Anglo-Saxon Teutonic goddess of spring and fertility. In France, Easter is known as *Pâques*, and all Romance language names for Easter are from *Pascha*, for "Passover".

## HE IS RISEN

The Easter story can be simply told: two days after Christ was placed in the tomb of Joseph of Arimathea and a big stone rolled across the entrance, Mary Magdalene, Mary, the mother of James and Salome, and "the other women" (the gospels differ on who was with Mary Magdalene) visited the tomb to anoint the body with spices, only to find the stone rolled away and the sepulchre empty. An angel sitting on the stone informed them that Jesus had risen (*see Easter: The Quem Quaeritis, opposite*).

## A DATE IN DISPUTE

Easter was first known as "Pasch", and the earliest references to it date from the 2nd century. Easter is a moveable feast, meaning that its date varies each year according to the lunar calendar (all of the other major Christian holidays follow the solar calendar). During the first centuries of Christianity, the correct date was disputed, but the First Council of Nicaea in AD 325 finally decreed that

*Above The unleavened bread of Passover has become in Catholicism the unleavened bread transubstantiated into the Eucharist. The bread is being made in this 15th-century detail from the Schocken Bible.*

Easter was to be celebrated the first Sunday after the 14th day of the moon (approximately the full moon) following the date of the spring equinox (assumed to be 21 March). Therefore, Easter can come as early as 22 March or as late as 25 April. The dates of other holy days, such as Pentecost, depend on the Easter date. Easter's date is linked to the Jewish celebration of Passover, because the Last Supper, three days before Christ's Resurrection, was a Passover Seder.

## CHRIST OUR LIGHT

After the darkness of the events of Holy Week, Catholics express their jubilation at the Resurrection in the traditional Easter vigil service. Near midnight on Easter eve, Catholics gather in a dimly lit church, symbolizing the darkness of Christ's tomb, and wait. Outside the church, a new fire is kindled and blessed. At midnight, priests light the paschal candle, marked with the Cross and the alpha and omega, symbols of Christ, from the new fire and process

*Left Andrea Mantegna's dramatic 15th-century painting of Christ's Resurrection is scripturally inaccurate – according to the Bible no man or woman witnessed Christ coming forth from the tomb.*

## EASTER: THE QUEM QUAERITIS

Four lines of dialogue beginning in Latin *Quem Quaeritis*, or "Whom do you seek?" were the genesis of the theatrical tradition of miracle and mystery plays that began in the 10th century. The Quem Quaeritis is a trope, or elaboration, of the part of the Easter liturgy that describes Mary Magdalene and "the other women" finding Jesus' tomb empty, with an angel sitting on the great stone.

*Whom do ye seek in the sepulchre, O followers of Christ?*
*Jesus of Nazareth, the Crucified, O heavenly ones.*
*He is not here; he is risen, just as he foretold.*
*Go, announce that he is risen from the sepulchre.*

The original adapted dialogue has come down to us in manuscripts from the monks at the 10th-century Abbey of St Gall and in actual stage directions written *c.*AD 965 by Bishop Ethelwold for Benedictine monks at Winchester. The original four-line vignette was performed, in Latin, by priests in the church sanctuary. Such dramatic renditions by the clergy of parts of the Easter liturgy were so popular that the subject matter was expanded to dramatize episodes from the New Testament and the lives of the saints. Responsibility for productions was removed from the clergy and taken over by the guilds of medieval towns, who performed the plays in English, with non-reverent elements.

*Above Mystery plays, adaptations of biblical scenes, were produced in public squares on moveable stages known as pageant wagons, as depicted in this 16th-century English illustration.*

into the dark Church, symbolizing the Resurrection of Christ our Light. Easter is also traditionally associated with the baptism of new converts to Christianity, and Easter vigil services often incorporate baptisms of new Catholics on this auspicious day. The custom of wearing new clothes at Easter derives from the fresh white robes worn by the newly baptized.

The association of light with Christ's Resurrection is also the symbolic basis of the sunrise services, a variation of the Easter vigil. Often held on a hilltop, the faithful wait to see the new light of dawn pierce the dim sky; after dawn, a mass is celebrated outdoors. Joyful Catholics may be greeted by their priest with the ancient traditional Easter greeting, "Christ is risen indeed!" The one greeted then replies with "And hath appeared unto Simon!"

*Right An Easter vigil opens with the kindling of a new paschal candle, a large white candle symbolizing the return of the light of Christ, which is relit throughout the year to mark sacred rites.*

# CHRONOLOGY OF POPES

SINCE ST PETER, THE FIRST POPE, THERE HAS BEEN AN ALMOST CONTINUOUS SUCCESSION OF POPES. THE FOLLOWING IS A CHRONOLOGICAL LISTING OF ALL THE POPES WHO HAVE HEADED THE ROMAN CATHOLIC CHURCH.

*c.*32–66 Peter
*c.*66–78 Linus
*c.*79–91 Anacletus
*c.*91–101 Clement I
*c.*101–109 Evaristus
*c.*109–16 Alexander I
*c.*116–25 Sixtus I
*c.*125–36 Telesphorus
*c.*138–42 Hyginus
*c.*142–55 Pius I
*c.*155–66 Anicetus
*c.*166–74 Soter
*c.*174–89 Eleutherus
*c.*189–98 Victor I
*c.*198–217 Zephyrinus
217–22 Callistus I
222–30 Urban I
230–5 Pontian
235–6 Anterus
236–50 Fabian
251–3 Cornelius
253–4 Lucius I
254–7 Stephen I
257–8 Sixtus II

260–8 Dionysius
269–74 Felix I
275–83 Eutychian
283–96 Caius
296–304 Marcellinus
*c.*306–8 Marcellus I
*c.*310 Eusebius
311–14 Miltiades
314–35 Silvester I
336 Mark
337–52 Julius I
352–66 Liberius
366–84 Damasus I
384–99 Siricius
399–401 Anastasius I
401–17 Innocent I
417–18 Zosimus
418–22 Boniface I
422–32 Celestine I
432–40 Sixtus III
440–61 Leo I
461–8 Hilarius
468–83 Simplicius
483–92 Felix III
492–6 Gelasius I
496–8 Anastasius II
498–514 Symmachus
514–23 Hormisdas
523–26 John I
526–30 Felix IV
530–2 Boniface II
533–5 John II
535–6 Agapetus I
536–7 Silverius
537–55 Vigilius
556–61 Pelagius I
561–74 John III
575–9 Benedict I
579–90 Pelagius II
590–604 Gregory I
604–6 Sabinian
607 Boniface III
608–15 Boniface IV
615–18 Adeodatus I
619–25 Boniface V
625–38 Honorius I

638–40 Severinus
640–2 John IV
642–9 Theodore I
649–53 Martin I
654–7 Eugene I
657–72 Vitalian
672–6 Adeodatus II
676–8 Donus
678–81 Agatho
682–3 Leo II
684–5 Benedict II
685–6 John V
686–7 Conon
687–701 Sergius I
701–5 John VI
705–7 John VII
708 Sisinnius
708–15 Constantine
715–31 Gregory II
731–41 Gregory III
741–52 Zachary
752 Stephen II
752–7 Stephen III
757–67 Paul I
768–72 Stephen IV
772–95 Hadrian I
795–816 Leo III
816–17 Stephen V
817–24 Paschal I
824–7 Eugene II
827 Valentine
827–44 Gregory IV
844–7 Sergius II
847–55 Leo IV
855–8 Benedict III
858–67 Nicholas I
867–72 Hadrian II

*Above* St Peter, the first pope, was traditionally supposed to have been crucified upside down, as in this fresco by Leonhard von Brixen, 1470.

872–82 John VIII
882–4 Marinus I
884–5 Hadrian III
885–91 Stephen VI
891–6 Formosus
896 Boniface VI
896–7 Stephen VII
897 Romanus
897 Theodore II
898–900 John IX
900–3 Benedict IV
903 Leo V
904–11 Sergius III
911–13 Anastasius III
913–14 Lando

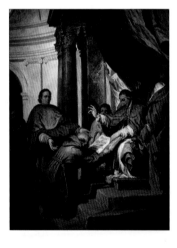

*Above* St Francis of Assisi presents the regulations of his new order to Pope Innocent IV in this 18th-century painting by Niccolo Ricciolini. Innocent IV was a strong pope, affirming papal authority.

*Right* Pope Clement V was responsible for moving the papacy to a new seat in Avignon, France, in 1305. This statue tops his tomb in Bordeaux's St André Cathedral.

**Above** *Pope Clement VII suffered being taken prisoner in 1527. Giuliano Bugiardini's portrait, c.1532, shows him six years later, in more dignified times.*

914–28 John X
928 Leo VI
928–31 Stephen VIII
931–5 John XI
936–9 Leo VII
939–42 Stephen IX
942–6 Marinus II
946–55 Agapetus II
955–63 John XII
963–5 Leo VIII
964 Benedict V (deposed)
965–72 John XIII
973–4 Benedict VI
974–83 Benedict VII
983–4 John XIV
985–96 John XV
996–9 Gregory V
999–1003 Sylvester II
1003 John XVII
1003–9 John XVIII
1009–12 Sergius IV
1012–24 Benedict VIII
1024–32 John XIX
1032–44; 1045; 1047–8
   Benedict IX
1045 Sylvester III
1045–6 Gregory VI
1046–7 Clement II
1048 Damasus II
1049–54 Leo IX
1055–7 Victor II
1057–8 Stephen X

1058–61 Nicholas II
1061–73 Alexander II
1073–85 Gregory VII
1086–7 Victor III
1088–99 Urban II
1099–1118 Paschal II
1118–19 Gelasius II
1119–24 Callistus II
1124–30 Honorius II
1130–43 Innocent II
1143–4 Celestine II
1144–5 Lucius II
1145–53 Eugene III
1153–4 Anastasius IV
1154–9 Hadrian IV
1159–81 Alexander III
1181–5 Lucius III
1185–7 Urban III
1187 Gregory VIII
1187–91 Clement III
1191–8 Celestine III
1198–1216 Innocent III
1216–27 Honorius III
1227–41 Gregory IX
1241 Celestine IV
1243–54 Innocent IV
1254–61 Alexander IV
1261–4 Urban IV
1265–8 Clement IV
1271–6 Gregory X
1276 Innocent V
1276 Hadrian V
1276–7 John XXI
1277–80 Nicholas III
1281–5 Martin IV
1285–7 Honorius IV
1288–92 Nicholas IV
1294 Celestine V
1294–1303 Boniface VIII
1303–4 Benedict XI
1305–14 Clement V
1316–34 John XXII
1334–42 Benedict XII
1342–52 Clement VI
1352–62 Innocent VI
1362–70 Urban V
1370–8 Gregory XI
1378–89 Urban VI
1389–1404 Boniface IX
1404–6 Innocent VII
1406–15 Gregory XII
1417–31 Martin V
1431–47 Eugene IV

**Right** *Pope Urban VIII was a temporal leader as well as a spiritual ruler, with his own coinage. This gold coin was produced in Avignon, France.*

1447–55 Nicholas V
1455–8 Callistus III
1458–64 Pius II
1464–71 Paul II
1471–84 Sixtus IV
1484–92 Innocent VIII
1492–1503 Alexander VI
1503 Pius III
1503–13 Julius II
1513–21 Leo X
1522–3 Hadrian VI
1523–34 Clement VII
1534–49 Paul III
1550–5 Julius III
1555 Marcellus II
1555–9 Paul IV
1559–65 Pius IV
1566–72 Pius V
1572–85 Gregory XIII
1585–90 Sixtus V
1590 Urban VII
1590–1 Gregory XIV
1591 Innocent IX
1592–1605 Clement VIII
1605 Leo XI
1605–21 Paul V
1621–3 Gregory XV
1623–44 Urban VIII

1644–55 Innocent X
1655–67 Alexander VII
1667–9 Clement IX
1670–6 Clement X
1676–89 Innocent XI
1689–91 Alexander VIII
1691–1700 Innocent XII
1700–21 Clement XI
1721–4 Innocent XIII
1724–30 Benedict XIII
1730–40 Clement XII
1740–58 Benedict XIV
1758–69 Clement XIII
1769–74 Clement XIV
1775–99 Pius VI
1800–23 Pius VII
1823–9 Leo XII
1829–30 Pius VIII
1831–46 Gregory XVI
1846–78 Pius IX
1878–1903 Leo XIII
1903–14 Pius X
1914–22 Benedict XV
1922–39 Pius XI
1939–58 Pius XII
1958–63 John XXIII
1963–78 Paul VI
1978 John Paul I
1978–2005 John Paul II
2005– Benedict XVI

**Left** *Pope Benedict XVI, who was elected pope after one of the shortest conclaves in Catholic history, must face the challenge of giving leadership to the world's Catholics in an age of increasing secularism.*

# RELIGIOUS ORDERS

THERE ARE A GREAT MANY DIFFERENT ORDERS WITHIN THE CATHOLIC CHURCH. BELOW IS A LIST OF THE MAJOR RELIGIOUS ORDERS AND THEIR FOUNDERS, ARRANGED CHRONOLOGICALLY.

*Above St Benedict of Nursia can be seen teaching his Rule to his monks in this 13th-century French illustration.*

## BENEDICTINES
The first great order of monks, founded by St Benedict of Nursia in 529.

## CARTHUSIANS
Enclosed order, including both monks and nuns, established by St Bruno of Cologne, 1084.

## CISTERCIANS
Reformist monastic order, founded by Robert of Molesme in 1098 and greatly expanded by St Bernard of Clairvaux.

## CARMELITES
The Brothers (and Sisters) of Our Lady of Mount Carmel, founded in the 12th century on Mount Carmel, Israel.

## TRINITARIANS
Order of the Holy Trinity, an order of priests, monks and nuns that was founded by St John de Matha in France in 1198.

## FRANCISCANS
Friars (Mendicant Brothers), founded by St Francis of Assisi in 1209.

## POOR CLARES
The Order of Poor Ladies, founded in Assisi, Italy, by St Clare with the help of St Francis in 1212.

## DOMINICANS
Friars, predominantly a teaching order; established by St Dominic in southern France in *c.*1215.

## AUGUSTINIANS
A group of monastic orders, incorporated as a "Grand Union" in 1256.

## CAPUCHINS
The Order of Friars Minor Capuchin, following a back-to-first-principles re-foundation of the Franciscans, started by Matteo di Bascio in 1520.

## THEATINES
The Congregation of Clerks Regular of the Divine Providence, known as the Theatines from their foundation in Chieti (Theate), Italy, founded in 1524 by St Cajetan.

## JESUITS
The Society of Jesus, founded by St Ignatius Loyola in 1534.

## URSULINES
Order of nuns, devoted mainly to the teaching of girls, established in Italy by Ste Angela de Merici in 1535.

## SISTERS OF LORETO
Order of nuns founded by Mary Ward, an Englishwoman in French exile, in 1609.

*Above St Bruno, founder of the Carthusian order, prays in the wilderness at Chartreuse, France, in this 17th-century painting by Nicolas Mignard.*

*Right A 14th-century sculpture shows St Bernard of Clairvaux, a leading Cistercian, carrying the chapel of Clairvaux, the abbey that he founded.*

*Above St Ignatius Loyola presented the rule book for his newly established Society of Jesus to Pope Paul III (1534–49), shown in this anonymous painting.*

## CONGREGATION OF THE MISSION
Also known as the Lazarists or Vincentians, this order of priests was established by St Vincent de Paul in 1624.

## DAUGHTERS OF CHARITY
Often referred to as Sisters of Charity, a congregation of nuns formed by St Vincent de Paul in 1633.

## TRAPPISTS
An order of monks and nuns, a Cistercian offshoot named for France's La Trappe Abbey, where their famous rule of silence was first introduced in 1664.

## LOVERS OF THE HOLY CROSS
Order of nuns, founded in 1670 in Vietnam and centred in the Far East.

## REDEMPTORISTS
The Congregation of the Most Holy Redeemer, who are missionaries to the poor; the order was founded in Italy by St Alphonsus of Ligouri in 1732.

## CONGREGATION OF CHRISTIAN BROTHERS
Commonly known as Christian Brothers, a congregation of lay brothers within the Roman Catholic Church, dedicated to educating poor boys worldwide; it was established by Edmund Ignatius Rice in Waterford, Ireland in 1808.

*Above Trappist monks perform their religious office at the Abbey Notre-Dame d'Aiguebelle, France. Prayer is an important part of their routine.*

*Above An Indian nun from the Missionaries of Charity ministers to Calcutta's poor. Founder Mother Teresa won international renown for the charity's work with the destitute.*

## SOCIETY OF MARY
The Marist Fathers (the Marist Brothers are an offshoot), an order of teachers and workers dedicated to the poor, founded by William Joseph Chaminade in France, 1817.

## LITTLE SISTERS OF THE POOR
Order of nuns dedicated to the care of the poor – especially the elderly – founded in France by Jeanne Jugan in 1839.

## SOCIETY OF AFRICAN MISSIONS
Founded by Melchior de Marion Brésillac in 1850.

## WHITE FATHERS
More formally, the Society of the Missionaries of Africa, founded in Algeria by the French cardinal Charles Lavigerie in 1868.

## MISSIONARIES OF CHARITY
An order of nuns established in 1950 by Mother Teresa of Calcutta to help the poor.

# Index

Page numbers in bold denote
illustrations.

Aachen 40; Palatine Chapel 40
abortion 58, 59
absolution 60, 61
Adam and Eve 50
adultery 57
Advent 45, 77, 81, **82**
Africa 32, 33
Alacoque, Marguerite Marie 69
Alexander III 93
Alexander IV 27, 93
Alexander VI 93
altar, the **42–3**; sacrament of **48–9**
Annunciation 72, 80
apostles 42, 52, 60, 68, 88; Apostles'
    Creed 72
archbishops 12
Ascension 81
Ash Wednesday 80, **86–7**, 88
Association of Papal Orders 35
Assumption, the 77, 81
Augustine 20, 27
Augustinians 20, 26, 94

baptism **50–1**, 75
Basilica of Our Lady of Peace (Ivory
    Coast) 41
Basilica di Santa Maria del Fiore 40
Benedict 20, 22, 94
Benedict XI 93
Benedict XII 93
Benedict XIV 93
Benedict XV 13, 93
Benedict XVI 7, 8, 13, 50, 67, 71,
    74, 79, 93
Benedictines 20, 22, 26, 28, 29, 31,
    91, 94
Bernadette 73
Bernard of Clairvaux 87, 95
bishops 8, 12, 13, 18, 19, 44, 52, 65, 74
Blessed Virgin see Mary
blessings **74–5**
brides of Christ **28–9**
Bruno 24, 94

Callistus I 92
canon law 13
cardinals 12; College of Cardinals
    8, 9, 12
Carmelites 26, 29, 94
carnival **84–5**
Carthusians 24–6, 94
Catechism, the **126–7**
Catedral Metropolitana Nossa Senhora
    Aparecida (Brasilia) 41
Cathars 73
Catholicism: Catholic Calendar 77,
    **80–1**; Catholic Year **76–91**; see also
    Church, the
celibacy 14, 15, **16–17**
Charlemagne, King 40
Christ: in the wilderness 86; see also Jesus
Christmas 45, 81, **82–3**
Church, the: early Church 52; hierarchy
    of **12–13**; institutions of **6–35**;
    marriage to **16–17**; see also
    Catholicism
Church of the Holy Sepulchre
    (Jerusalem) 65, 77
churches and cathedrals 42–3
Cistercians 25, 29, 94
Clare of Assisi 30
Clement V 92, 93
Clement VI 93
Clement VII 93

Clement VIII 93
clergy: married clergy 17; vestments
    of **44–5**; see also archbishops;
    bishops; priests
Communion 4–5, 46, 49, 53, 55, 68
confession **60–1**
confirmation **52–3**
contemplative monasticism **24–5**
contraception 58–9
Councils: of Lyons 26; of Nicaea 90;
    Vatican II 17, 41, 46, 63, 65
creeds: Apostles' Creed 72; Nicene
    Creed 47
Crucifixion of Christ 60, 70, 71, 89

deacons 12–15, 18, 44, 47
disciples 68
divorce 57
Dominic 33, 35, 73, 94
Dominicans 26, 27, 35, 94

Easter 45, 60, 80, 88–9, **90–1**
Escrivá, Josemaría 34, 35
Eucharist, the 19, 36–8, 42–6, 48–9,
    53, 55, 60, 63, 64–5, 75
extreme unction 63

Fabian 92
fasting 86–7
feast days 69, 78–9, **80–1**
Francis of Assisi 20, 30, 92, 94
Franciscans 14, 20, 26, 33, 94; Secular
    Franciscans 35
friars 26–7; Black Friars 26–7;
    Friars Minor 94; Grey Friars 26;
    White Friars 27
funeral services **64–5**

Gabriel the archangel 73, 81
Galileo Galilei 10–11
Gelasius I 8, 92
Gennaro 79
Good Friday 65, 71, 80, 89
gospels: Holy Gospel 47, 51, 72, 75;
    John's Gospel 43, 89; Luke's Gospel
    73, 83; Matthew's Gospel 16, 68,
    73, 83, 87, 88
Gothic churches 38, 39
Gratian, Emperor 86
Gregory I (the Great) 35, 82,
    86, 92
Gregory IV 92
Gregory IX 93
Gregory XI 93
Gregory XV 93

Henry VIII, King 57
heresy 73
hermitages 24–5
Hippolytus 86
Holy Days **78–9**, 80–1
Holy Father, the **8–9**
Holy Matrimony **54–7**
holy orders **18–19**, 74
Holy See 10, 11, 13
Holy Spirit 50–2, 64, 66
holy water 47, 51, 74
Holy Week **88–9**, 90
homosexuality 58
Honorius III 93

Ignatius Loyola 21, 95
Immaculate Conception 81
India 21, 31, 95
Innocent III 93
Innocent IV 92, 93
Innocent VIII 93

Januarius 79
Jerusalem 38, 65, 77
Jesuits 21, 39, 94
Jesus 80, 81; birth of 82–3; death of 60,
    70, 71, **88–9**; the Jesus Prayer 66;
    Resurrection of 45, 46, 65, **90–1**;
    temptation of 86; see also Christ
Jewish Temple (Jerusalem) 38
Jews 66
John 8, 43, 52, 71, 89
John XXIII 34, 93
John the Baptist 50
John Bosco 27
John Paul I 9, 93
John Paul II 9, 13, 17, 29, 31, 32, 34, 40,
    41, 46, 59, 65–7, 70–2, 93
Joseph 55, 80, 82
Joseph of Arimathea 71, 90
Judaism 90
Judas 71, 85, 88, 89
Julius II 93
Justinian I, Emperor 13

last rites 62, **63**
Last Supper 42, 46, 89, 90
Lateran Councils see under Councils
Lateran Treaty (1929) 10
lay groups **34–5**
laying on of hands 19
Lent 45, 60, 70, 84, **86–7**
Leo I (the Great) 92
Leo III 40, 92
Leo X 93
Leo XIII 22, 93
Lincoln Cathedral 38, 39
Litany of the Saints 18, 19
Little Sisters of the Poor 30–1, 95
liturgy: of the Eucharist 48–9, 55; of the
    Hours 22–4; liturgical year 77; of the
    requiem Mass 64; Tridentine 65; of
    the Word 46–7
Liverpool Metropolitan Cathedral 39, 41
Lord's Prayer 73
Lourdes 45, 73
Luke 73, 83

Marcellinus 92
marriage 54–7; annulment of 57;
    married clergy 17; mixed marriage 55
Mary 24, 48, 55, 71, 72–3, 80–2
Mary Magdalene 90, 91
Matthew 16, 68, 73, 83, 87, 88
Maundy Thursday 80, 89
mendicants **26–7**
Michael the archangel 81
missionaries **32–3**; in Africa 32–3; in the
    Americas 32–3; in India 31;
    Maryknoll 33; Missionaries of
    Charity 30–1, 67, 95; Missionaries of
    La Salette 33; Missionaries of the
    Poor 32; Missionaries of the Sacred
    Heart 32
music, church: requiem Masses 65
Mysteries: Glorious 72, 73; Joyful 72, 73;
    Luminous 72; Sorrowful 72

Nativity, the 82–3
Nicholas IV 93
Nicholas V 11, 93

Opus Dei 34–5
orders, religious see religious orders
ordination 15, **18–19**

Palm Sunday 80, 88
Passover 90
Paul 16, 79–81; Paul's Epistles 46

Paul II 84, 85, 93
Paul III 95
Paul V 93
Paul VI 8, 13, 17, 93
penance and reconciliation **60–1**
penitence 46; penitential meditations
    70–1
Pentecost 45, 52, 69, 77, 81
Peter 8, 10, 12, 13, 40, 42, 52, 68, 71, 79,
    81, 88, 92
pilgrimage 73
Pius VII 93
Pius IX 35, 69, 70, 79, 93
Pius X 53, 93
Pius XI 93
Pius XII 34, 69, 93
Poor Clares 20, 29, 30, 94
popes **8–9**, 12; in Avignon 92;
    chronology of **92–3**; election of 8, 9;
    papal infallibility 8–9
prayer **66–7**; Eucharistic Prayer 48–9
priests 12–13, **14–15**, 16–28, 43, 44–5,
    47, 60–5, 74
Protestantism 17, 39

Raphael the Archangel 81
Reformation, Counter- 39
relics, sacred 42
religious orders **20–1**, 22–31, **94–5** see
    also by name of order
Resurrection 45, 46, 65, **90–1**
Robert of Molesme 94
Rome **10–11**; Bishop of 8
rosary, the **72–3**
rules (of religious orders) 20, 22, 25, 35

sacraments, living the **36–75**
Sacred Heart Cathedral (Bendigo) 69
Sacred Heart of Jesus **68–9**, 81
St Asaph Cathedral (Wales) 43
Saint-Etienne-du-Mont (Paris) 39
St Patrick's Cathedral (NYC) 42
St Peter's Basilica 6–8, 10, 40
saints days 45, 77–81
Scriptural Way of the Cross 71
Shrove Tuesday 77, 80, 84
sick, annointing the **62–3**
sign of the Cross 74, 75
Simon of Cyrene 71
sin 61; mortal sins 60; venial sins 60
Sistine Chapel 9, 10
Sixtus IV 93
Sixtus V 85, 93
Society of Apostolic Life 21
Society of Jesus 21, 39
Stations of the Cross **70–1**
Sylvester I 35, 92

temptation (of Jesus) 86
Teresa, Mother 30, 31, 67, 95
Teresa of Ávila 28
Thérèse of Lisieux 29
Trappists 25, 95; Trappistines 31
Urban II 95
Urban VI 95
Urban VIII 79, 93

Vatican 6–7, **10–11**; Vatican Councils see
    under Councils; Vatican Library 11
Venice 84
Veronica 71
vestments **44–5**
vows 20–1; of celibacy 15; of obediance
    15, 19

White Fathers 95
women in the Church **28–31**